THE KNOWLEDGE ENGINE

The
Knowledge
ENGINE

HOW TO CREATE FAST CYCLES OF
KNOWLEDGE-TO-PERFORMANCE
AND
PERFORMANCE-TO-KNOWLEDGE

Lloyd Baird and
John C. Henderson

BK

BERRETT-KOEHLER PUBLISHERS, INC.
San Francisco

Berrett-Koehler Publishers, Inc.
450 Sansome Street, Suite 1200
San Francisco, CA 94111-3320
Tel: (415) 288-0260 Fax: (415) 362-2512 www.bkconnection.com

Ordering Information
Quantity sales. Special discounts are available on quantity purchases by corporations, associations, and others. For details, contact the "Special Sales Department" at the Berrett-Koehler address above.
Individual sales. Berrett-Koehler publications are available through most bookstores. They can also be ordered direct from Berrett-Koehler: Tel: (800) 929-2929; Fax: (802) 864-7626; www.bkconnection.com
Orders for college textbook/course adoption use. Please contact Berrett-Koehler: Tel: (800) 929-2929; Fax: (802) 864-7626.
Orders by U.S. trade bookstores and wholesalers. Please contact Publishers Group West, 1700 Fourth Street, Berkeley, CA 94710. Tel: (510) 528-1444; Fax: (510) 528-3444.

Printed in the United States of America
Printed on acid-free and recycled paper that is composed of 50% recovered fiber, including 10% post consumer waste.

Library of Congress Cataloging-in-Publication Data
Baird, Lloyd.
   The knowledge engine : how to create fast cycles of knowledge to performance and performance to knowledge / Lloyd Baird & John C. Henderson.—1st ed.
      p. cm.
   Includes bibliographical references and index.
   ISBN 1-57675-104-X
   1. Knowledge management. 2. Performance—Management. I. Henderson, John C. II. Title
HD30.2 .B347 2001
658.4'038—dc21   2001025513

First Edition
07 06 05 04 03 02 01   10 9 8 7 6 5 4 3 2 1

Interior Design & Illustration: Gopa Design & Illustration
Copy Editor: Sandra Beris
Proofreader: Henrietta Bensussen
Indexer: Paula C. Durbin-Westby
Production: Linda Jupiter, Jupiter Productions

Contents

Dedicated to
Marty and Coleen
for their support and inspiration.

PERFORMANCE

Preface

KNOWLEDGE

IN EARLY 1992, we began a small project at the request of General Gordon Sullivan, then chief of staff of the U.S. Army. He was in the midst of a major restructuring initiative that was occurring as a result of the end of the Cold War and would ultimately lead to the U.S. Army cutting its size and budget in half. One central tenet of his efforts was that the army had to be smarter and faster, not just smaller. He viewed the army's ability to leverage knowledge creatively as key to reaching that objective. He invited us on a whirlwind tour of bases, operations, and training facilities. Our assignment was to evaluate the usefulness of the army's Center for Army Lessons Learned and the related training efforts for improving its operational efficiency and strategic capability. Although the army approached organization and leadership problems from a different perspective than we did, as we worked together we discovered more and more convergence. We found an army whose effective use of physical assets, although still critically important, did not determine its success as much as did its effective use of knowledge assets.

Throughout our careers we have been involved with corporations, helping them figure out how to be more effective. At Boston University we work with many of these corporations in institutes and roundtables including the Human Resources Policy Institute, the Executive Development Roundtable, the Center for Enterprise Leadership, the Asian Management Institute, the Leadership Institute, and the Systems Research Center. Each is sponsored by twenty to thirty corporations dedicated to working together to find solutions to common problems. They define the issues, we provide the research capability. Most recently many of our partners have been coping with the shifting economy. Everyone recognizes that the world is getting faster and more complex. The issue is how to respond. We shared with our corporate partners what we learned in our work with the U.S. Army and discovered that many were grappling with the same issues. A group of organizations proposed that we work with them to investigate how to create and leverage knowledge assets. We formed the knowledge management working group with the help of the U.S. Army, BP, General Motors Corporation, Xerox Corporation, Lucent Technologies, Zachry Construction Corporation, J. Sainsbury, and Kraft Foods, Inc. Our purpose was not to focus on the technology of knowledge management or even its theoretical merits but rather to better understand the link between knowledge and performance.

This book reports on what we found. We have chosen the title very carefully: *The Knowledge Engine: How to Create Fast Cycles of Knowledge-to-Performance and Performance-to-Knowledge*. Knowledge is the engine that will drive organizations forward in the future. Leaders will have to know how to create and leverage knowledge assets. The engine has two cycles. During the production cycle, knowledge is driven into performance. During the strategic cycle, performance is the source of knowledge. This knowledge engine also works differently depending on its context. Although organizations share ideas, tools, and best practices both internally and externally, these assets must be uniquely applied. But we discovered that the underlying principles are surprisingly consistent across contexts. Therefore, this book is organized around those principles. We present examples and describe tools and practices but always with the caution that they must be adapted to the particular case and in adherence to the principles.

During the process of putting this book together, we were over-taken by the e-business wave. Soon that wave will pass; the next wave is already forming. Knowledge management will no longer be a specialized field but rather the responsibility of leaders. Use the e-business and knowledge management tools to produce business results, but recognize that the next wave is coming quickly. It is even more knowledge intensive and will place an even higher pre-mium on understanding the principles of leading in a dynamic economy.

We too are already preparing for the next wave. We have extended the Leadership Institute and the Systems Research Cen-ter into the new areas we must understand to assume a leadership role in the future. Once again our partners have pushed us forward. We are working with those in other disciplines—finance, market-ing, operations, human resources, information technology, and economics—to drive even higher levels of payoff. Our partners have made very generous financial contributions and more impor-tantly provided us access to their organizations and shown a will-ingness to continue our work together.

Together, we have founded the Institute for Leading in a Dynamic Economy. Again we chose the title very carefully: *leading* because we can affect what happens to ourselves and our organi-zations; *dynamic economy* because the only constant in the future will be change. The challenge for the twenty-first century is to be even faster and smarter in coping with the changes. The institute is an international initiative to coordinate the efforts of leading universities and corporations. It is funded by significant grants and will involve both theoretical and applied researchers and practi-tioners from around the globe. Currently, applied research focuses on visualization, information technology strategy, the emerging role of the CIO, the role of learning in corporate strategy, and the leadership requirements of the new economy.

We will continue to work with partners willing to discover together. We will continue to report what we find. Most impor-tantly we will continue to have fun doing it together. This book is a report of where we are now. We provide the concepts and tools we have discovered along the way. We present them for one purpose: to help you drive higher levels of performance.

Lloyd Baird
Boston, Massachusetts
January 2001

John C. Henderson
Boston, Massachusetts
January 2001

Using Knowledge Assets to Drive Performance

OUR BOOK is not about knowledge management, data ware-houses, or e-commerce. As important as these phenomena are, they are only pieces of a more fundamental puzzle, a puzzle that requires new ways of thinking and acting. Our book is about how to succeed in the knowledge-intensive economy into which we are all being thrust. New information capabilities are emerging at a dizzying pace, redefining industry structure and management processes (Quinn, 1992). The truly competitive products and services are not found in the traditional sectors alone; more and more of them are found at the intersections. In fact, traditional definitions of indus-try sectors are blurring as companies are woven together in an intri-cate web of relationships linked by information. Cost and quality, the twin pillars of competitive advantage in the industrial age, are now the norm rather than differentiating factors. In the new econ-omy, speed and knowledge have emerged as the keys to success (Fine, 1998). Speed is evident not only in shorter product life cycles but also in the rapid merging of organizations to form whole new entities that information technology makes possible. Knowledge embedded in products and business processes now drives what can be created and delivered to customers (Davenport and Prusak, 1998; Nonaka and Takeuchi, 1995).

It would also be a mistake to assume that the new knowledge-intensive economy is just about Internet companies. It is equally about the transformation of leading companies driven by information technology. Companies are finding business success by blending opportunities in digital space with valuable assets from their traditional operations (Evans and Wurster, 2000). Witness, for example:

⇨ The transformation of Westinghouse from industrial giant to media and broadcasting leader

⇨ The repositioning of FedEx as the airline of the Internet

⇨ NBC's creation of NBC Interactive to blend television with the World Wide Web

⇨ Enron's redefinition of its value proposition in the power industry by using newer risk-management techniques

⇨ The reinvention of American Express, Merrill Lynch, and Fidelity in the tumultuous financial services market by leveraging the power of the Internet

⇨ General Motors's deployment of Onstar as a strategy for the next incarnation of automobiles by connecting them to a larger network that both delivers information and entertainment and enhances their performance

We do not see a battle between dot.coms and brick-and-mortar businesses. Rather, we see the leveraging of global connectivity and pervasive computing power by all firms as they attempt to innovate and redefine the rules of competition.

The Changing Context

The distinguishing characteristics of the new economy are the links across customers, units, and organizations that are made possible by information technology and the subsequent falling costs of transactions. Networked technologies are creating new ways for buyers and sellers to connect (Hartman, Sifonis, and Kafdor, 2000).

The traditional middleman is being eliminated as both customers and suppliers are linked through financial or market exchange intermediaries. Yet new intermediaries arise—some call them *infomediaries*—that create new buyer-seller connections. New, cheaper channels of distribution are emerging in all areas of the economy. Customers have new ways to explore on their own the products and services they want. Organizations are being redesigned to enable the freer flow of products and services. As consumers gain more information and more options, they gain more control. Consider, for example, four characteristics of the new economy that have changed forever the relationship between the customer and the supplier.

Personalization

Customers are demanding that products and services fit their unique needs. The trends toward flexible manufacturing and what is often called mass customization that began in the 1980s and 1990s are continuing. Customers determine what they want and when. Direct delivery is increasingly available to all customers in twenty-four hours. Customers expect the seller to know them, know their preferences, and reward them for repeat business by personalizing every contact experience. The world of financial management is moving very quickly to the point where the bank, stockbrokers, and investment counselors are available any time, anywhere the customer is. For example, log onto Fidelity's Web site—**www.fidelity.com**—and click on the Powerstreet feature to see what you can do. The information revolution that provides everyone information about pricing and features is simply increasing the pace of change.

Dynamic Pricing

Pricing decisions are one of the most closely held decisions in a firm, and yet the market is the ultimate arbiter of price. Pricing decisions change based on time and place as products and services are constantly updated and shifted. The Internet has linked everyone and everything together so intricately that negotiations once conducted face to face between two parties are now conducted dynamically across multiple suppliers and customers. Although online auctions were initially used as a distribution channel to liquidate excess inventory, they are now being used as a sales medium for a wide range of products and services. Log onto **www.esteel.com/**, for example. A basic commodity, steel, may now be bought and sold over the Internet through auctions.

Connectedness

We live in a world where everything is becoming connected. Businesses are connecting in new and interesting ways with customers, customers are connecting back with businesses, customers are connected with other customers—and devices are connecting with other devices. The smart Coke machine of today can communicate with its suppliers and schedule its own refill, or it can change prices in response to local shifts in demand. The smart kitchen moves information across appliances so that the refrigerator "knows" what is being used: the cook can plan a menu and the kitchen will order the appropriate supplies to be delivered to the home at a specified time (see **www.kraftkitchen.com/** for an example). Products are becoming smart as they talk with each other, but the information embedded in any given transaction is often more valuable than the goods or services that are exchanged in the transaction. The extreme level of connectivity also permits the emergence of new organizational forms. Sometimes referred to as *virtual organizations*, these organizational entities are a network of companies that combine their core capabilities in ways that serve their customers.

Customer Communities

The role of customer communities has also changed in this new economy. Previously, in the industrial economy, consumers were essentially independents. The firm influenced what they knew about the firm, its products and services, and its other customers. The information was presented in a way that made the firm's products and services look as favorable as possible. But now the rules have changed. Customers talk with other customers on a global as well as a local scale. People who read similar books talk with each other online (see **www.amazon.com**). Health care networks are emerging that link not only pharmaceutical companies with patients but patients with other patients and doctors with other doctors (see **www.merckmedco.com**).

The context of business becomes ever more complex as these same types of relationships extend to other units and organizations. Stockholders have quicker, more dynamic, personalized information and investment opportunities. Business partners are much more integrated and connected. Virtual networks emerge where hierarchies previously existed.

The Search for Answers

In the face of these new realities, we wanted to discover what it takes for a business to succeed. How can an organization get faster, create the new knowledge it needs quickly, and stay even more tightly linked with its customers, partners, stockholders, and employees? We decided that academic institutions—in their traditional incarnation—were too slow in developing knowledge, and businesses are too busy keeping up with the ever-increasing pace of change to allow them to step back and learn from their experiences. In many organizations, the staff specialists—who are traditionally responsible for discovering and implementing the new ways—have been downsized and those who remain are so focused on the short term that they have little time or ability to develop new models and practices. We needed a collaborative effort of discovery, a collaboration that merged the strategic needs and fast-cycle response of the firm with the knowledge-generating capability of academic institutions.

In 1990 we began working with a leading group of companies at Boston University's Systems Research Center, where together we defined issues and researched solutions for the new business context. In 1996 a few of these companies approached us and wanted to become even more tightly connected. They all had launched knowledge management initiatives and were concerned that it be more than just the next fad. They also had the sense that they were moving too slowly. As one executive put it, by the time they analyzed, set targets, implemented, and reached the destination, "*There* was not there anymore." The world was moving too fast. They needed to discover a way to learn quicker and apply what they learned faster. Speed was achieved only if those performing were also responsible for the learning and knowledge, not if they delegated to a training organization, consulting firm, or university. Knowledge had to be gleaned from the performance process itself. And knowledge had to feed back into performance. Knowledge-to-performance, performance-to-knowledge and back again quickly. Hence our logo:

Nine organizations came together to search for answers over a four-year period: Boston University, the U.S. Army, BP, General Motors Corporation, Xerox Corporation, Lucent Technologies, Zachry Construction Corporation, J. Sainsbury, and Kraft Foods, Inc. We met quarterly, were linked together electronically, and spent lots of time in one another's facilities. We climbed oil rigs in England, ate sushi in San Francisco, and explored new technologies in Boston. This book presents a summary of what we learned.

We had a good base from which to begin. These organizations are noted for their information technology and knowledge management capabilities. But they had another common bond as well: they were concerned about performance. In fact, at one of the initial sessions of our group in Detroit, Vince Baraba, chief technology officer at General Motors Corporation, summed up the company's concern with the title of his presentation, "Why I Hate Knowledge Management." His and everyone's goal at the very beginning was to affect performance, not build a library. Paula Snead, Executive Vice President of Marketing at Kraft, summed up her concerns this way: "Kraft does not need to produce more information; we need more insight." Kraft already had the capability to track sales by SKU, aggregating that information to identify trends in purchasing and hone marketing strategies. Snead could see Kraft entering a world where everyone had access to that same information—all of Kraft's competitors, down to the smallest corner store. There would be no unique competitive advantage in having that information; instead, the competitive advantage would have to come from the insight extracted from information and the quickness with which it could be applied. If information is at parity, with everyone having it, then knowledge would offer the competitive advantage.

Back to Basics

Our partner organizations were also early adopters of e-commerce strategies, forming Web sites, linkages, and relationships both internal and external to the firms using emerging technology. But they had the same concerns about e-commerce as we did—they could see the capability to do business on the Web spreading like wildfire. Eventually—and it is happening faster than even they anticipated—"e-capability" would also be at parity. Having the Web site, linkages, and relationships would not provide a competitive advantage. Because everyone would have them, they would become the price of admission to the game of business. The competitive advantage would shift to the ability to extract learning and knowledge from the interactions that the Web facilitates and to use it to drive action and business decisions.

We quickly got back to basics. The questions to be explored were not how to mount a knowledge management initiative, adopt an e-commerce strategy, or implement new information technology.

Instead, we wanted to find out how to innovate, serve customers better, drive higher levels of performance, cut costs and increase efficiency, and adopt the correct strategies and implement them—in other words, run the business. The sustainable competitive advantage was to be as it has always been, to identify the right customers and to deliver value to them quicker, cheaper, and faster. That has not changed. So, what has changed?

Knowledge: The Critical Asset

The early part of the twentieth century was dominated by those who knew how to control physical assets. To honor those who have had an impact on our lives and how we do business, *Fortune* magazine chose Henry Ford as businessperson of the century. Indeed, Ford was the man who invented the assembly line, exploited the idea of vertical integration as a way to gain control of physical assets, and paid people not as little as possible but fairly so they would remain loyal and productive. Ford knew how to leverage physical assets.

In the world today knowledge is becoming the key to competitive advantage. The popular press would have us believe that the whole world has gone crazy over electronics, technology, and the Internet. And they are right. The Internet, even in its infancy, is dominating corporate decision making. The knowledge about customers that is obtained when they buy something is as important as the money they spend. Information technology is becoming even more important in defining who we are and how we work. Just as we did with physical assets, we now need to know how to create and leverage knowledge assets.

A knowledge asset is created when the know-how or experience of individuals can be used by someone other than those involved in its creation. Such an asset can be systematically redeployed in a way that continually creates value (Davenport and Prusak, 1998). Historically, firms leverage their knowledge assets by leveraging their human resources. To redeploy key knowledge, firms redeploy people. Although this tried-and-true method works and will continue to be used, it has its obvious limits. Even in a world of video-conferences and e-mail, you can only time-slice your key experts so fine. At some point, they burn out. So in our work together we sought to find ways to augment the use of individual interaction to share knowledge. We sought to understand how knowledge could be acquired and redistributed independently from its source.

Building a Two-Cycle Engine

Our main question as we began our work together was this: "How can we create and leverage knowledge assets?" The metaphor of an engine became a useful way to think about how to organize our work. An engine both creates power and uses power to accomplish something. How could we build a "knowledge engine" that would both create knowledge assets and use them to drive performance?

In a dynamic world the relationship between strategy and execution changes. It is no longer enough that the two be in alignment. Instead, the challenge is to sustain the alignment. Strategy must move into the world of real time, a constant interaction between what is done, what is learned, and what is planned.

Strategy must guide execution and set up the conditions for learning.

Execution must produce results and capture learning that informs strategy.

Success in the new economy still requires an organization to implement the right strategy efficiently. But strategy becomes an experiment (Quinn, 1992). And the experiment works only if implementation becomes both a chance to perform and a chance to learn. Every action, every interaction with a customer, every job completed, every opportunity must not only contribute to performance but also to knowledge. Knowledge thus becomes an asset that can be leveraged to drive performance.

Our challenge, then, was to build a two-cycle engine, with one cycle continually producing the knowledge that drives performance and the other cycle continually orienting performance and knowledge capture in the right direction. Thus, the engine would have a *production capability* and a *strategic capability*.

The Production Capability

In our fieldwork we located best practices—such as the U.S. Army's after action reviews and BP's peer assists—that effectively produced knowledge assets and promoted knowledge sharing. We will describe these practices more fully in later chapters; but suffice it to say here that they are both techniques to capture knowledge directly from and during the performance process. We saw knowledge-sharing initiatives, such as Xerox's Eureka Project that resulted in significant and measurable performance increases. As we continued our search we gradually defined the knowledge engine's production cycle: *to acquire*, *to structure*, and *to target*.

Acquire

The acquisition stage of the production cycle involves the processes and techniques used to capture and codify knowledge so it can become an asset. By acquisition we mean the ability of those involved in an event to surface and capture usable knowledge based on their experience. Acquisition has not only a capture but also a time dimension. Knowledge can be acquired:

⇨ Before an event, using simulations and experimentation
⇨ During an event, using after action reviews
⇨ After an event, using post hoc analysis

Knowledge gained before and during an event is the most valuable. Our ability to learn from what has happened decreases as more time elapses. We forget, become more biased, and re-create events in ways that prevent accuracy. Most fascinating and helpful are advances in simulation techniques that offer opportunities to gain "experience" before going "live." We can create knowledge assets before events actually happen, which gives us a powerful opportunity to produce knowledge efficiently and effectively. As we will discuss in more depth in Chapter 3, knowledge acquisition is not just about codification. It is also about increasing the likelihood that others will use what is learned.

Structure

We use the verb *structure* rather than *store* for the second stage of the production capability to emphasize the broader range of design choices (rather than merely technology choices) for making knowledge assets available to potential consumers. By structure we mean to synthesize, consolidate, and organize knowledge so that people want it and will come and get it. The elegance of the database and extent of the information are irrelevant if no one uses them. Thus the two questions that frame leaders' challenges in structuring knowledge are: How can what is known be organized to increase others' motivation to come and get it? How can what is known be organized so it is easily accessible?

At this stage, leaders must decide how to create a means of access for the knowledge consumer and how to sustain the ongoing maintenance and administration of this asset. As we will see in Chapter 4, at this stage we not only determine who has access and how but also begin to establish how people integrate knowledge into their own performance processes.

Target

Finally, consistent with our emphasis on performance, the third stage of the production capability is to *target*. Sometimes you cannot wait for people to come and access the knowledge that has been created. It may just be too crucial. Sometimes you have to deliver the knowledge to them. You have to push it into their performance. At this stage we address a "push" rather than a "pull" strategy. Targeting means identifying the knowledge consumers and packaging the knowledge asset so it is most usable by them. Targeting does not wait for knowledge consumers to come and access the knowledge base, but proactively pushes knowledge to them. By targeting we mean packaging and delivering the right knowledge, to the right people, at the right time, in the right format. Acquire, structure, target: a tight cycle that produces and quickly applies knowledge.

The Strategic Capability

After establishing the requirements on the production side, we were left with the problem of ensuring that our efforts would be applied in ways that support the organization's strategic goals. The knowledge engine needs an engineer, or director. It needs to produce knowledge that drives performance consistent with the firm's or the unit's strategy. We do not have time or money to capture everything we can and hope it helps us do better. We have to gather the specific knowledge that drives performance. We observed that many of the successes achieved by our firms had a strategic equivalent to the production cycle. There were two cycles—one focused on action, the other focused on the strategic direction of the unit or firm—and both worked together to drive performance.

Focus

As we will see in Chapter 2, during the *focus* stage we not only use strategy to identify where to direct investments in future knowledge assets that are consistent with organization strategy but also establish the basis for motivating people to share and use those assets. By focus we mean to provide just enough of the right knowledge, at the point of decision and action, to change people's abilities and motivation, to produce results.

Reflect

Equally important is to *reflect*. At this stage the leader, regardless of his or her organizational level, looks across events to consolidate, integrate, and develop a higher-level perspective that allows him or her to challenge the current direction, ways of thinking, and business models. By reflection we mean:

⇨ Validating what we are seeing in one unit by comparing it with what is happening in others
⇨ Integrating what we are seeing across many units to develop a higher-level view

Heifetz (1994) refers to this as "being on the balcony." When you are on the balcony you gain a vantage point from which to get a better overall picture of what is happening. On the balcony you can be both in and out of the game, to manage the ebb and flow between action and knowledge.

As we will describe in Chapter 6, if you do not see the overall picture, you will be doomed to chase incremental production cycle improvements that will gradually lose their value. Although investments in knowledge assets at the local level may pay short-term dividends, they will not drive you to reinvent both process and products at the strategic level, which is necessary in a turbulent world. Together *focus* and *reflect* provide a push and pull on strategy. They not only use strategy to direct knowledge initiatives but provide the knowledge that will drive the strategy itself.

Dynamic Alignment

As we have already suggested, although the engine has two cycles they are inherently interactive. The production capability provides the daily, short-term experience and learning that feeds into and becomes the basis for the strategic activities of focusing and reflecting. Meanwhile, the strategic capability guides and defines the knowledge-producing activities of acquiring, structuring, and targeting. The two cycles not only build capability but feed off each other to power a learning engine that moves faster and faster but continually helps to refocus the strategic orientation of the firm. (See Figure 1.1.)

Figure 1.1

The Dynamic Alignment of the Knowledge Engine

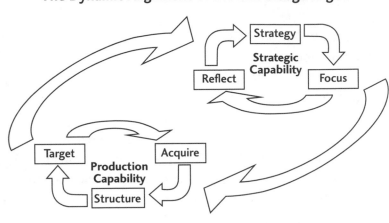

The Guiding Principles

Our efforts to share our insights and apply existing theory in our small and very diverse group of companies posed some interesting challenges. We now had the framework for the knowledge engine. But what about the concerns of Vince Baraba, Paula Snead, and our other partners, and the charge they gave us? What we found was that too often tools, processes, and techniques gleaned from one organization did not fit the others. A process that worked at Xerox would not work for the U.S. Army. We found ourselves looking for a reasonable basis to generalize and share without removing the complexity of the local context. Indeed, therein lies the fallacy of many knowledge efforts. They focus on the tools rather than on what makes them work. Our partners wanted us to take it to a deeper level. They could adapt, develop, and apply the tools and processes depending on their situation. They wanted help in understanding "how" and "why." They wanted us to help them discover *the guiding principles*.

As a result, this book does not prescribe solutions, provide fixed tools, or suggest the "correct" process. Each firm has its unique challenges, and more importantly, its situation is constantly changing. Thus, rather than offer a solution or a method, we attempt to identify principles that can be used by any firm to figure out its own solutions. Our colleagues phrased it this way, "We need a compass and an understanding of where true North is. We do not need a detailed path. Each of us will have to work that out in the context of our business." Decisions about how to implement the knowledge engine have to be made at the local level. Anything else is fundamentally at odds with the business environment, the new economy, and the need for quick cycle links between what we know and what we do. Principles guide but do not restrain adaptation.

A principle is *a statement that is intended to guide the future actions of individuals in a way that will increase performance*. Stephen Covey (1990) views a principle as a basic compass that guides individuals in their personal and organizational lives, the bedrock of their behavior. Others have used the concept to affect the decision-making process of the firm. For example, Broadbent and Weill use the term *maxim* to describe both business and information technology principles. "The maxims draw on a firm's mission or strategy statements. Their purpose is to articulate an agreed-on position in a form that executives can readily understand and act on" (Broadbent and Weill, 1997, p. 81). Designers of complex systems have long recognized the value of decision-oriented principles. A common principle guiding database design is, "Data should be stored in one and only one place." Of course, such a principle can be implemented in many ways (local choice). Thus, a principle is not a standard or a rule to be followed without question nor a solution or a policy that dictates correct functional behavior. Rather, it is a guide, and each individual will make choices, ideally in ways that are consistent with the principle. Perhaps most important is that when choices are consistent with the principle, performance improves.

We used five criteria to frame our principles and ensure that they were guides for developing and adapting tools and processes, rather than rigid dogma:

Principles Are Purposeful

Principles are intended to affect behavior and performance in a significant manner. As such, principles are in themselves decisions—decisions about how to set the compass to guide the organization in a particular direction. A principle may be contrasted with a belief. A belief is a strongly held conviction but it may not affect the behavior of others. For example, I may believe that the Internet will change the nature of business, but this belief is, in itself, a weak source of guidance. It is not a purposeful statement. Thus, a principle is based on beliefs but beliefs are not principles.

Principles Are Generalizations
of Causal Relationships

As a mechanism to guide behavior, principles have an underlying means-ends model. Implicit in the previously mentioned principle of "one source of data" is that it will reduce cost, improve quality, or have some other impact on performance. The choice to follow a principle is, in effect, a design choice. It steers you in a direction that is hypothesized to affect performance.

Principles Are Objective Statements
That Can Be Measured

This characteristic separates principles from values. Efforts to ground the actions of an organization through shared values will clearly influence behavior. But values can rarely be empirically assessed. In contrast, if a principle's effect can be measured and evaluated, then there can be feedback and learning.

Principles Are Context-Independent

Principle implies a causal means-end relationship that is situationally independent. Of course, no principle is completely independent of its context. However, the stronger the principle the more applicable or valid it is in a broad range of circumstances. For example, a principle of knowledge acquisition is, "Capture lessons learned as close to the action as possible." This principle guides the methods used to collect knowledge assets. The principle is that the validity of the knowledge gained by the "soldier in the foxhole" is linked to the likelihood that this knowledge will influence the behavior of others. Further, this principle is valid in a wide variety of settings, so it has value as a decision-making guide.

Principles Assume a Local Decision-Making Process

The creator of a principle must imagine a social system in which free will, and hence, local decision making, is the norm. Thus, principles are distinguished from policies or rules. A rule dictates behavior, removing local decision-making power. In contrast, when you follow a principle you make the decision and take accountability at the local level. A principle seeks only to narrow the range of alternatives. It can be very influential, but never definitive. An organization operating with a coherent set of principles can move responsibility and accountability down the organization while striving to ensure these local decisions are made cumulatively in ways that enhance its overall performance.

Principles and Choices

So, with principles come choices. How an organization will apply a principle varies based on the nature of the organization, its leadership style, and the context within which knowledge assets are created and leveraged. Leaders must make choices based on what they are trying to accomplish. In the succeeding chapters we will frame the choices and give examples of how others have made them and explain the tools and techniques. However, it is important not to get caught in what we refer to as the "get me one of them" trap: An executive visits a supplier and sees a great way to leverage knowledge from one team to another, a staff assistant attends a speech by a leading business figure extolling the virtues of the firm's new e-commerce initiative, a division head is impressed by a conference presentation on the latest technology that highlights the great cost savings accrued. All of a sudden they have to "get one of them."

That is not what leaders do. Instead, they make choices that fit their objectives—based on principles. This book provides you with examples and gives you guidance—but you will have to choose. Rarely can the tools and techniques applied in a totally different context be lifted and directly applied. They have to be adapted, modified, and adjusted in order to work.

Our Objective and Our Audience

In the following chapters, we will explore the components of the knowledge engine in greater detail. We will explain each component, highlight the alternative approaches available to leaders who wish to use the component, illustrate each approach with examples taken from our research, and finally, clarify the principles that we saw in use at the companies we studied. In the end, we hope that readers will gain a basis to get into the action of creating and leveraging the knowledge assets.

Finally, a word about our audience. We were careful to use the word *leader* rather than *top executive* throughout the book, because the responsibility to create the knowledge engine lies with everyone who heads up a unit, manages an accounting team, coordinates a project, or simply tries to work productively with others. All are leaders responsible for creating and leveraging knowledge assets. To the extent they do, they and their units will be able to keep up with the dynamic economy in which we all live and work.

Focus

Beware the Field of Dreams

JUST BECAUSE you build a knowledge base does not mean they will come. Just because it is elegant does not mean they will use it. They will come if it helps them perform. They will use it if it helps them achieve. You cannot simply collect everything possible and hope that they find what they need. While he was leading the knowledge team at BP, Kent Greenes phrased it this way, "We don't need a just-in-case knowledge base, we need just-in-time knowledge." The pressure for performance is too high and things change too fast for anything else. Your employees and customers need what they need when they need it.

By *focus*, we mean to provide:

⇨ Just enough of the right knowledge
⇨ At the point of decision and action
⇨ To change people's abilities and motivation
⇨ To produce results

A company may choose to focus on cutting time and costs in a product development process. It may want to find out why one region outperforms another. It may focus on launching a new product in a way that allows it to learn quickly in one country and adjust what it is doing in another. Or it may simply get a group of people to focus on critical performance areas and learn from their own experience. However they do it, the first challenge for leaders is to provide a focus for knowledge initiatives.

"What" and "How" Knowledge

With so much information available, where do you start when you want to focus? At a fundamental level, performance-based knowledge is about *what* and *how*. Knowledge about *what* is reasonably straightforward and easily collected, so it tends to dominate most information systems.

Knowledge about *what* may be complex and may even involve significant detail, but it is essentially descriptive. It is not surprising that organizations and individuals focus on *what* data. This information is stored in warehouses, libraries, and even the World Wide Web. Indeed, the most daunting challenge for the leader has more to do with setting limits on *what* knowledge rather than finding new ways of capturing it. Consider all the information your organization collects and stores. Most of it is probably information about *what*: What market are we trying to expand and how are we doing it? What is the optimal lot size for inventory replacement? What are the characteristics of the customers buying our products? Where is our inventory stored? How much money do we have? Where are all of our trucks? How many people do we have? The list is endless. The size of such an information base is unlimited—and so is the cost!

Knowing *what* is only a small first step in finding the right focus. The next step is to understand *how*. This is more complex but often more important for improving performance. *How* information can actually help us understand what we need to do rather than simply tell us where we are. Know-how resides in processes, experiences, and relationships. To gain know-how, we must often run experiments and learn from action. We can seek out experts to tell us what to do; sometimes they can even tell us how and why. But often our context is so different from theirs that we have to learn how and why from our own experience. We have to learn for ourselves the unique applications that produce results in our jobs. Furthermore, experts provide no competitive advantage. Everyone has access to the same experts. Knowledge from the outside moves so quickly, it becomes a commodity and we lose the competitive advantage. Competitive advantage comes only from knowledge about how things work based on our own experience.

How information has two components: relationships and context. First, it is necessary to understand relationships. How does the new advertising campaign affect potential customers? If we move our storage facilities, how will it affect costs? Understanding these relationships requires different processes than those required to capture descriptive *what* data. This kind of knowledge comes through action and it is acquired with experience, experimentation, or analysis over time.

Second, it is necessary to understand the context in which the action takes place. Knowledge about *how* is often quite sensitive to *where*. How does the new advertising affect the people who buy in New York versus those in Chicago? The more complex the relationships, the more important the context. The age-old saying, "You had to be there," is quite appropriate when it comes to the knowledge of *how*. Context is the background or environment that a full description should capture. But any context with so rich a description would require abstraction. Regardless of the descriptive medium, this abstraction process results in the loss of information. The challenge is to retain sufficient detail to allow future consumers to use the knowledge in a productive manner but at the same time not overwhelm them with what is available.

This becomes even harder to do when you try to explain how things happen over time. Context becomes a dynamic concept and must be described as such. This is a difficult task requiring quite different skills and methods than when you attempt merely to describe an event at one point in time. For example, think about the difference between a snapshot and a movie. The context—the background and the images that surround the events you are trying to see—is important in both, but it is much more difficult to depict them well in the latter format.

Sports provide another analogy—take football, for example. When you're watching a game, knowing that the score is 7 to 14 does you little good unless you also know that the New York Jets are 7 and the New England Patriots are 14. You are even better able to understand what is happening if you know this is the half-time score. If you owned the New York Jets and were trying to improve the team's performance you would need to know even more details. Which plays led to the score? What were the weather conditions? How large was the crowd, and did their excitement and cheering affect the game? Even a high school coach knows that a video of the last game will provide far richer information on it than statistics, even if they are detailed statistics that are specific to each player. At the professional sports level the amount of data available reaches the absurd. The information is available to anyone who can pay the fee. You can learn any player's batting success against any pitcher in the league and with any supporting team. You can track the improvement of your players versus others over time. The data available are unlimited. Yet sports team owners and managers still hire scouts to go to games to watch players in action. They still review the videos of games and plays. They know that even detailed descriptions miss the interaction between each player and his or her environment. How did the player react under pressure? Can the player elevate his game when necessary? How good was the competition? The questions are endless, and the subtleties often make the difference between simply good performance and excellent performance.

When an organizational leader wants to improve performance, *how* information is absolutely critical. It does little good to know what happened if you don't know how it happened. You need deep *how* knowledge in a few important areas rather than superficial *what* knowledge scattered across the organizational landscape.

When you are looking for information on both relationships and context, the amount and scope of it is infinite. You have to stay focused or your field of dreams will grow so large that it will simply collapse under its own weight.

Four Steps to a Clear Focus

Logically, the *what* and *how* knowledge needed will be determined by a company's strategic orientation, its performance objective. When you focus—just like when you calibrate a microscope—you go through a series of steps that gradually reduce your scope of view until you can efficiently see the knowledge that will produce results. Our work indicates that taking four key steps can help companies focus effectively.

Focusing Knowledge Initiatives
Step 1: Focus on a core capability.
Step 2: Identify the knowledge gap.
Step 3: Define the key performance drivers.
Step 4: Establish clear ownership.

Focus on a Core Capability

Organizational performance is ultimately judged by the market. It is defined at the moment a customer makes a choice. What value do you create and deliver to the customer? How do you deliver this value? Capabilities determine how well you can answer those questions. A capability, in essence, is the ability of a firm or a unit to deploy and use its resources—people, relationships, equipment, money, and so on—in a distinctive manner that is valued by its customers (Quinn, 1992). A simple concept, yet one that is quite difficult to articulate in a way that allows for meaningful action.

N. Venkatraman (1999) distinguishes between three types of capabilities: core, necessary, and support. A *core* capability is one that differentiates a firm from its competition. This is the essence of who you are and what you can do better than anyone else. Federal Express's core capability is its logistics and tracking systems that allow it to pick up a package where the customer is and take it to where the customer wants it. If Federal Express does not do that well, it does not matter how great its finance or personnel department is. Furthermore, the company can leverage this core capability in many ways. For example, it can help another company design its logistic systems. A core capability allows a firm to give customers what they perceive to be unique value. A focus on core capabilities can be likened to the first level of calibration for a microscope.

Many of BP's activities are linked together in order to find, drill, extract, process, and sell oil and gas. The question for this company was where to focus. BP managers did an analysis and decided that the actual mechanics of running the oil rig was important but gave the company no distinct advantage; in fact, others could do it better. They decided to form partnerships and outsource these activities to Schlumberger and other large construction firms that know how to run rigs. Today 90 percent of the people on a BP oil rig are not BP employees. They work for the subcontractors hired to do the job. The remaining 10 percent include the foreman and the drilling rig managers who make sure the subcontractors' performance is up to standards and worry about capturing the knowledge that will drive corporate performance. Thus BP focuses on its core and outsources everything else.

BP offers other examples of focusing as well. The company set as one of its strategic objectives a very high standard of safety. In the oil business, much is driven by cost. However, industry accidents not only cause human tragedies but also are very costly. A rig may have to be shut down for investigation and corrective action. Today, BP is the best in its class in safety and is continuing to invest in this capability both to drive down costs and to save lives. Another key strategic objective for BP is to lead in the area of environmental impact. It aspires to have zero impact on the environment in all that it does—quite an objective for a company engaged in oil drilling and processing. Pursuing excellence in environmental impact has yielded significant new knowledge. Now the questions are how to leverage that knowledge in the corporation, use it for competitive advantage in the marketplace, or become partners with others by transferring the knowledge to other companies and charging for what BP has learned. The question becomes how to use this core capability to create new service offerings and build a new business.

Necessary capabilities are those that are unique to an industry but do not necessarily differentiate a firm. At BP, knowing how to run an oil rig is a necessary capability but it offers no competitive advantage. The advantage lies not in the operations per se but in the design of the system that allows multiple suppliers to collaborate effectively as they run rig operations.

Consider another example. In the pharmaceutical industry, product shipments must be tracked in order to ensure that a firm maintains the ability to recall any given production batch at any given time. As a result, supply chain management processes are quite unique to the industry. However, firms do not attempt to differentiate themselves based on this capability. They could have the greatest product shipping and tracking system of any pharmaceutical company and it would do them very little good if their research capability could not produce a blockbuster product.

A *support* capability is what all organizations must have if they are to survive. Basic accounting processes are a good example of a support capability. Human resources is another. Such functions only add value by enhancing the ability of the corporation to deliver on its core and necessary capabilities.

Now recognize how the importance of capabilities changes based on the value proposition to the customer. If you are the Bacall and Conniff accounting firm and your purpose is to provide accounting services for small- to medium-size businesses in Boston, accounting is your core capabiiity. If you are an executive recruiting firm, recruiting is your core capability. The nature of the core capability is determined by how the firm delivers value to the customer.

In summary, a core capability is one that differentiates a firm from its competition. It defines who the company is and what it can do better than others in the customer's perception. At Merck, a core capability is product development and introduction. Support and necessary capabilities are important, but by doing them well Merck simply gains parity with others. Today, firms often outsource these activities in order to focus on their core capabilities. By identifying your core capabilities you begin to hone in on the specific areas where performance pays off for knowledge initiatives.

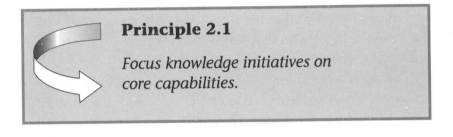

Principle 2.1

Focus knowledge initiatives on core capabilities.

Identify the Knowledge Gap

Once you define your core capabilities, you have narrowed your focus to those few areas where learning can have a real impact. Before launching any initiatives, however, there is a critical test you can take to help you determine if the effort will be worth the time and money required: that is, you can identify the extent of the knowledge gap. This is the second step in the focus stage.

A knowledge gap is the difference between what a unit or group knows and what they need to know to perform better. A significant knowledge gap can take many forms, but most often it occurs at an organizational boundary or when massive changes are needed. Thus, we see the following:

1. The gap may arise if teams or functional units do not share knowledge. One team does something well, but has no mechanisms for improving the performance of others.

2. The gap may occur across organizations engaged in a common process—for example, suppliers in a supply chain—if those upstream know things that those downstream should know and could use, but do not.
3. The gap may occur if one part of the firm innovates but does not communicate this innovation effectively.
4. The gap may occur as changes in the environment or competition require the organization to alter its processes and structure. The new knowledge needed can only be captured from experience.

Organizations should not spend their time, energy, and money in those areas that will not give them payoffs. The critical question is this: "Assuming we are successful in finding and/or sharing knowledge, what is it worth?" Creating and leveraging knowledge assets requires an investment, and as with any investment, should yield a return. Articulating the knowledge gap will sharpen the focus of the knowledge initiative, provide measures that can be used to assess progress, and perhaps most importantly, establish the basic incentive for participation.

Generally, in our research we have found that the biggest payoff comes from sharing knowledge across units. Rather than investing money in generating new knowledge, the focus should be on leveraging what you already know. Find those units that are performing better and ask the simple question, *Why*? Then spend your time and energy consolidating, synthesizing, and transferring what that group has learned. Often money spent generating new knowledge simply adds to the variability in performance. The good get better, but the average and the poor continue doing what they have always done and achieving the performance levels they have always achieved.

Here's an example. According to BP, oil drilling operations can be measured in terms of dollars per 10,000 feet, and the faster you can drill 10,000 feet the cheaper the cost. There is a big payoff if the organization reduces costs continually. At BP, drilling teams are responsible for repetitively drilling wells in specific oil fields. As these teams learn to work together and become more familiar with the characteristics of their assets (the oil fields), their drilling speeds improve. Figure 2.1 illustrates the type of performance data and subsequent learning curves for two teams drilling in different assets—Team A and Team B. Each team's efficiency is measured in terms of the cost of drilling 10,000 feet. BP's analysis of its teams across assets clearly identifies a significant knowledge gap. Managers can ask a simple question, "What is the payoff if we can get all the teams performing at the level of our best team?" Of course, the answer is a huge improvement. The best teams can and will generate new knowledge (that is, Team A moves from A1 to A2). Such learning is and will continue to be rewarded. However, the value of sharing knowledge across teams (moving the organization to an established high performance capability, or Team B moving closer to Team A) offers a higher potential return for knowledge initiatives. The biggest payoff comes when other teams leverage what one team already knows.

Why can't everyone do as well as the best? There may be many reasons: different geographic areas present different problems, different teams work together more or less efficiently, and different work processes are involved in drilling. All of these reasons are valid, but if you consider them carefully you will see that they do not negate the value of knowledge sharing. Even if local conditions are the cause of some differences, much can be gained by simply getting others to use knowledge that some in the organization already have.

Faced with the challenge of getting everyone to perform as well as the best, BP launched its Drilling Learning Project initiative in an effort to increase knowledge sharing at a community level. Representatives from the drilling community identified key areas in which learning would be important. Then they selected a champion in each area. The champion's responsibility was to cut the knowledge gap by identifying key learnings, validating the information, and making it available to the rest of the community through a Web site.

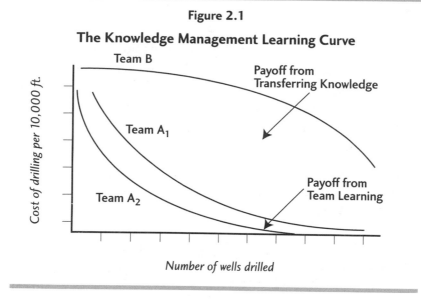

Figure 2.1

The Knowledge Management Learning Curve

Number of wells drilled

Areas for knowledge sharing ranged from those that were well understood, such as safety, to areas that were very tacit, such as goal setting or team building. Specific data were shared that improved productivity—estimating costs, for example—and new techniques and processes were also discovered. BP also engaged its key suppliers and partners in creating and leveraging knowledge assets that improved overall performance. The capability to learn, create, and leverage knowledge assets not only added to the success of BP but also became a key responsibility of all leaders. Over the years, this has become one of its core capabilities for delivering value to customers.

The list on the following page shows the categories in which BP identified knowledge gaps. Rig start-up was found to be a critical area in which BP could save considerable expense if it could handle it faster, cheaper, and more safely; Brian Hay is the champion who is responsible for collecting and disseminating knowledge in this category. Chris Lockyear is the champion for risk management; Chris Brown for safety. These individuals have become key links to the larger community of oil drillers.

Knowledge Categories for Drilling Operations

⇨ Contracting
⇨ Incentives
⇨ Performance management
⇨ Team building
⇨ Data management

⇨ Goal setting
⇨ Rig start-up
⇨ Tech awareness training
⇨ Well design
⇨ Learning

Thus, before a knowledge initiative is undertaken, the critical test is to identify and assess the knowledge gap. Is the gap large enough to justify the expenditure in time and money?

Principle 2.2

Before investing, determine the performance payoff of closing the knowledge gap.

Focus on the Key Performance Drivers

Once core capabilities have been identified and the payoff has been quantified, it is time to identify those few performance drivers (PDs) that determine the firm's ability to deliver each core capability to the customer (Rockart, 1979). Much as with the concept of critical success factors described by Rockart, the process of defining these performance drivers helps to clarify how knowledge sharing will affect performance. The question asked in the PD process is quite simple: What are those few actions that enhance success in this core capability? In essence, the PD process is the 80/20 rule applied to organizations. It recognizes that all work processes are incredibly complex. And yet experienced professionals can often pinpoint one or two critical processes that are the heart and soul of an effective capability. It is in this area that the biggest payoff lies.

Consider, for example, the workings of a regional salesforce. The sales manager has just received quarterly reports that sales targets are not being met. Of course, this type of information—information on goal achievement—is certainly important because it alerts management that there is a problem, but it does not provide information on how to take action. A PD analysis might suggest that key activities are to get more "face time" with the customer or to target presentations so each customer is exposed to fewer but more relevant products. If these were actual PDs, an effective knowledge system would share innovation strategies for gaining access to key decision makers, what was learned at this event, and so on. Over time, this process of innovation can lead to significant improvement. When combined with appropriate outcome or goal accomplishment data, each sales team improves, and, it is hoped, approaches the efficiency frontier.

Each button on the BP Web site names a performance driver. These were identified by members of the drilling community because they were drivers of performance and because there existed a knowledge gap that could significantly affect the efficiency and effectiveness of that driver.

Identify the performance drivers of your core capabilities. What are those few actions that have the greatest impact on success? By identifying the key performance drivers you can further limit the scope and sharpen the focus of your efforts to learn from experience and capture the key lessons that will improve performance.

Principle 2.3

Identify and use performance drivers to further refine and determine the priorities for knowledge initiatives.

Establish Clear Ownership

The final step of the focus phase is ownership (Prokesch, 1997). Who will be responsible for getting it done? In this step an implicit or explicit contract to achieve results from a knowledge initiative is drawn up. Firms vary in the degree of formality associated with this commitment process. In some cases, the agreement is a verbal one, perhaps supplemented by a project's objectives or goals statement. The advantage of an informal process is that learning does not take on a bureaucratic character. Work by Peter Senge and others on learning organizations stresses the need for sharing behavior to be a natural part of work, not something that must be dictated or forced by the hierarchy. A common complaint, even when efforts to focus are made, is that attempting to create knowledge simply leads to large repositories of documents, data, and lessons that no one uses. The challenge for the leaders is not to dictate the day-to-day activities of each individual but rather to provide a clear and unambiguous message about the objective, which is to improve performance. Creating and leveraging knowledge is useful only if it improves performance. Without that focus, knowledge management will simply become the next fad to come and go, and it will go very quickly. Nothing lasts if it does not produce results.

Some organizations have found that establishing a more formal performance contract helps keep a performance orientation. A performance contract is a mechanism used to ensure that a project or position in an organization is well thought out and that expectations are clear and concise before the project begins. The key components of such a contract include definition of the stakeholders in the initiative, establishment of leadership roles, definition of expected outcome, benefits, and a general time line on which to establish these results. In the end, the contract simply puts down on paper the areas of focus, the critical few questions to be answered, who will be doing the collection, and how and what the expected results are. Tool 1 presents guidelines for knowledge contracts; it is based on the contract used by BP.

Tool 1
THE PERFORMANCE CONTRACT

1. *Background:* This section of the contract explains what parties are involved and how the project or position came to be, and offers a brief summary of the expected outcome.

2. *Stakeholders:* The stakeholders include the employees who are directly involved in this project, as well as consultants. They also include the departments that will benefit directly and indirectly from the project.

3. *Knowledge area focus:* This section identifies which areas of knowledge will be focused on in order to get maximum leverage on business performance.

4. *Execution:* Here the project is broken down into phases that build on each other. Each phase includes specific tasks that must be met before you can move on to the next phase.

5. *Deliverables:* Deliverables are the clearly defined expected outcomes. Exactness and proper planning should ensure the desired results.

6. *Benefits:* The specific benefits of the project are directly correlated with the deliverables. Benefits may include reducing costs, streamlining systems, or enhancing products.

7. *A plan:* The plan defines the schedule of dates by which each of the tasks defined in the execution section of the contract will be accomplished.

8. *Accountabilities:* The persons held accountable for each section of the project and their roles are set down here.

9. *Budget:* The budget is broken down to show the required costs of the project, including salaries, travel expenses, equipment, and so on. It also identifies which accounts are responsible for the costs of the program.

10. *Risks:* A list of the risks involved in endorsing the project helps the participants to be aware of what problems to avoid and helps management to understand possible shortcomings in execution.

Although the extent to which the different divisions of BP use this formal contract varies, the intent associated with the contracting process—to achieve a clear performance focus—is widely accepted. As a result, the link between efforts to leverage knowledge and the internal incentive system is direct. BP does not pay people to capture a lesson learned. It pays people to find and recover oil more efficiently. To the extent that knowledge sharing drives this performance objective, incentives to participate become very strong. Linking knowledge-sharing behavior to performance provides the foundation for sustaining the knowledge initiatives over time. There are no questions about what the focus should be.

Principle 2.4

To drive implementation, use performance contracts to establish clear ownership.

Moving Forward

This chapter set out the first, and perhaps most controversial, component of our knowledge engine concept (see again Figure 1.1). By emphasizing the focus we run the risk of narrowing a company's knowledge initiative in ways that could actually hinder its ability to create and leverage intellectual capital over time. Could we not, through this process, focus on the wrong things? Do we not run the risk of stifling "out-of-the-box" innovation? We accept that risk. In return, we expect to achieve two key objectives.

First, we can more quickly launch the firm into a knowledge initiative with a shared commitment to improve performance by doing so. In this way, we directly address the fundamental issue of usage. If you build it, will they come? Yes, they will come because it will help them perform.

Second, we establish a basis for assessment and further investment. The measure of success is not the creation of a repository. The measure of success is improved performance. In essence, a focus establishes a direct link between knowledge sharing and performance. This process of assessing and adapting over time will help make the knowledge-sharing process dynamic. It will be enhanced by the leader's role during the *reflection* activity discussed in Chapter 6. Because the leader can focus the firm to mobilize it to take action *and* can use the same focus to assess results, the risk of taking this step is well worth it.

Acquire

Learn As You Go

ONCE YOU HAVE A FOCUS, the next challenge is to acquire as much knowledge as possible as quickly as possible to guide action. By *acquire* we mean to surface and capture usable knowledge based on personal experience of an event. Typically, companies capture knowledge through postproject reviews, customer research, strategic audits, and analysis of experiences. Looking back is always valuable in understanding what has happened and providing the foundation from which to project what will happen and what to do in the future.

For our purposes, however, acquiring also has a time dimension. Because of the speed with which decisions must be made, the complexity of relationships, and the rate of change in the new economy, the context within which we must make decisions and guide action is different. The past is not as good a predictor of the future as it used to be. We cannot predict as well what people will want or do. The most we can do is make our best guess and then be able to sense quickly what is working and be adaptable enough to adjust. In this world, we cannot wait until the project is done, the assignment is completed, or the quarter is ended to capture what we are learning (Slocum, McGill, and Lei, 1994). We have to decide and act faster than that. The longer we wait to sense what is happening the less relevant our knowledge becomes. We have to learn as we go.

The human brain is a marvelous mechanism, but it is not built to learn quickly from experience. It does not keep an accurate running record of activities, situations, or transactions that can serve as a basis for sensing what is happening and responding. Nor is it designed to provide people with an accurate view of the world. Instead, it filters and sifts information and selectively explores details and scenarios. We all have a remarkable ability to pay particular attention to what we want and disregard the rest. We interpret things to our advantage by screening out what we do not want to hear and digesting information that is familiar and anticipated. This creates a dilemma.

Searching for Ground Truth

Research has shown that the best way to learn in such a fast-moving world is from experience. But the pace of change and the pressure for performance creates a sense that we cannot take the time to sort through our own biases and figure out what we are learning. The greater the pressure for speed, the more we have to learn on the job while we are performing, but the less time we have to do anything but get on with the next task. In good faith and with proper intentions we always vow to get back to it later, but we never do. Meanwhile, the further away from the experience we get, the less accurate our perceptions and conclusions.

The only way to resolve the dilemma is to search for what the military refers to as *ground truth*: the knowledge and learning of the person in the foxhole during the battle (Sullivan and Harper, 1997). In business terms, those responsible for performance should also be made responsible for learning. Every job should be not only a chance to perform but also a chance to experiment and learn how to perform better. The closer an individual is to the action the more likely he or she is to have valid information and the more likely others in the organization are to believe and use what he or she discovers. If the lessons cannot be learned right there on the spot, they need to be learned as close to the event as possible. The cycle time from when we do something, capture what is learned, and apply it back into action must be shortened. Thus, we are best served when learning becomes part of the performance process.

Another way to insert learning into the performance process is to go for quick-win prototypes. Identify a limited area where an idea can be tried out. Try to improve performance and see what happens. Risk a little and learn a lot. For example, Merck implements quick-win prototypes to test its products and roll out ideas. The U.S. Army rolls out new concepts in one unit and then builds on the success by rolling them out to other units. The key is not to wait. The motto that captures this philosophy is: "Get on with it— learn and adjust quickly."

Principle 3.1

Make those responsible for performance responsible for learning as well.

Learning While Performing

Unfortunately, simply doing something adds very little to one's knowledge. Experience provides a very rich, timely, and relevant set of information (Daudelin, 1996). But the true payoff comes when the learning is captured and the knowledge is applied. Every experience, good and bad, can be a learning event if approached properly. Failure is an opportunity to learn how *not* to do something. This is a seemingly obvious concept, but it is hard to implement. As Horst Abraham points out in his work on high performance, it is amazing how often people who fail keep doing the same thing over and over, actually expecting to see different results (Abraham, 2000). If you want something different you have to *do* something different.

Success is an equally important learning opportunity that is often overlooked. We get caught up in the euphoria of accomplishment and forget that two jobs must be done. Success is only half of the objective; learning from that success is the other half. Learning from experience follows a sequence: you know what you are trying to learn, you have the experience, and you capture what you learn so you can do better next time—a common sense sequence that is often ignored. A benchmarking team goes out to find good examples when they could have found the very best examples and most valuable learning through their own experiences. A student arrives at the laboratory and runs an experiment but learns nothing. A musician practices scales endlessly and puts in the time but because she does not evaluate her own performance, her performance does not improve. A career development session is held but no attempt is made to capture learning from the person's own experience. A manager is assigned to a foreign country but not given any way of capturing his learning while abroad. The examples of forfeited learning opportunities are endless. We are not used to acquiring knowledge from our experiences. We need structured tools and approaches to help us make that a natural part of our performance process.

The Kind of Knowledge to Seek

As a process, acquiring knowledge during experience may seem straightforward. All you really have to do is write down truly insightful thoughts while something happens, right? Or perhaps write down everything you see and worry about what it all amounts to later. Wrong! Neither approach will do much good. The real challenge is to capture *relevant* knowledge.

Is the knowledge you have captured likely to be used? Is it actionable? Can you do something with it? Those are the relevant questions. General Gordon Sullivan, recently retired U.S. Army Chief of Staff, says, "A lesson is not learned until behavior changes" (Sullivan, 1998). If the knowledge will have no impact on what is done and how well it is done, then why bother to collect it? This leads to a problem: the person using the knowledge, not the person collecting the knowledge, is the one who defines its relevance. The issues and situations I face determine what is relevant for me. As I launch a new product in France, I will face a set of issues that might be totally different from those you faced when you launched the same product in China. But how are you to know that before the fact? You have to do the best you can, and hope it helps others in the future.

Given this dilemma, it is not surprising that a common approach is to collect everything possible, just in case it might be needed. This approach leads to *scope creep*, which is the tendency to add more and more to the knowledge base. Avoid that, and keep the scope down. Remember the focus. You are trying to build a just-in-time—not a just-in-case—knowledge base.

When to Look for Knowledge

When do you look for knowledge? This might seem like a silly question with an obvious answer. If you are going to learn from experience, you look after the experience. This is the traditional answer. There are tools and techniques designed for learning after an event. Postproject reviews and retrospective analyses are all designed to help us capture as much learning as possible after an event is over. They all provide valuable insights, but as we have seen we need to drive the acquisition of knowledge as much as possible into the performance process. Historical reviews are often just too late.

Look Before

One way to get more learning into performance is to simulate performance and learn as much as possible before taking action. You do not have to live through an experience before you learn from it. Risk a little bit of time and money before acting. You can use experiments, role-plays, what-if analyses, walk-throughs, and information on what others have done. The military is well-known for using war games as a training method, but the games also help them learn how people act and react. For example, each year in the hills of Kansas, the U.S. Army conducts a game that it calls Prairie Warrior, a training and experimentation exercise. It is a massive war game simulation involving three thousand troops. Before they begin, the commanders identify specific training objectives: What should the troops learn?

At the same time, the army uses the simulation to test out new technologies and processes. The digital battlefield will be the next generation. On a digitized battlefield, everyone and every piece of equipment has a global positioning system (GPS) that is read by satellite and fed into the field computers that everyone else has. The advantage is simple: each person knows exactly where the others are and the direction in which they are moving. This is a tremendous advantage that every commander in every battle has wished for. Those involved in digitizing the battlefield have hypothesized that it will not only increase the collective knowledge during action but also the speed of decision making and reaction time.

The army did not want to wait for a real engagement to test out what digitizing would do to the decision-making process, the chain of command, and the speed of reaction and movement. They decided to test it out in the simulation. In Prairie Warrior, the army put a ground positioning system on all the soldiers and equipment in one set of troops to see how well they would perform against another set. They performed so well that they halted the exercise after only two days. A valuable lesson was learned on the impact of new technology before actual battles were fought (Baird and Henderson, 1997).

Simulations, role-plays, virtual reality techniques, and what-if analyses are not unique to the military. Business schools use cases and simulations to mirror the real world, law schools have mock trials, medical schools train students by letting them operate on cadavers, and pilots crash many airplanes in the simulator before they are allowed to take their first real plane into the air. These tools are used to capture knowledge before action takes place because certain things are just too costly and risky to try the first time in live action.

Still, we need to offer two precautions at this point. First, most organizations do not get everything they can from simulations. Too often they view them simply as training events and do not follow up with experimentation and what-if analyses as they should. By passing up these valuable opportunities, organizations lose a lot of the leverage they could gain from learning before the action. Second, the closer to the action the simulation, role-play, or what-if analysis is, the more likely the lessons learned will be applied in action.

Sainsbury, the large grocery chain with stores in England and the northeastern United States, carried out a rehearsal for the millennium. Mark Venables, the executive responsible for knowledge management and organizational transformation at Sainsbury, explained what the rehearsal was about (Venables, 1999). Three events that would happen toward the end of 1999 needed to be anticipated and a response to them practiced. The first event was a solar eclipse that would be initially visible in northern England in early fall. This well-publicized occurrence was such a draw that all the hotel rooms and campgrounds were booked nine months in advance. So many tourists in the area at one time were bound to affect normal buying patterns. The second noteworthy event was the parties that would be held to celebrate the new millennium. Finally, since both Christmas and New Year's Eve fell on Friday, people would take a full week to a week and a half of time off. During this period, they could be expected to eat differently than when they were working. With these three events happening over a four-month period, demands on grocery stores would be very unpredictable. A store that did not have the bottlenecks and kinks worked out in advance would not have enough time to adjust once the rush began. Venables and his team developed a one-day practice run. Executives came together and used what they knew to figure out what would happen to their own supply chain under different scenarios. Based on the results, they made adjustments and were ready early on.

Look During

The other option to drive more learning into the performance process and shorten the knowledge cycle is to capture learning during the action. Recently, a group of welders working the day shift on a metal tower decided to grapple with a problem on their own. The problem was that they would climb to their section of the tower to begin work only to discover that the night shift had worked on the same welds. "You start looking around and you see that a weld might look completed and you're wondering whether or not it has been tested, or if anything has to be done to it," said one welder (Deacon, 1998, p. 3). In order to obtain that information, the welders had to climb back down the tower, locate the foreman, and ask him. The foreman would have to find the quality inspectors to get the answers and then relay them back to the welders. The process was a waste of a lot of valuable time and money. The welders decided to get everyone together and ask them a few simple questions. As a result, they suggested that a notation be put right on the weld itself. The simple solution was to tag the weld, "saying that this has been tested, or it's OK or it's not, so you don't have to hunt down the foreman on it" (Deacon, 1998, p. 3). Action was immediate. By the next day, the notations were on the welds. The payoff was tangible; time and money were saved. The lessons learned were documented and shared at a daily supervisors' meeting. The supervisors then took that information and shared it with their own teams. Capturing the learning during the performance process prevented mistakes and raised efficiency to a higher level. The bottom line is to learn before or as close to the action as possible.

> ## Principle 3.2
>
> *In order to maximize timeliness and relevance, shift your knowledge-capture efforts to before and during an event.*

Who Should Look for Knowledge?

The obvious next question is, "Who should look?" Do you look for the lessons learned in your own experience or do you invite someone else to analyze what has happened and capture the lessons learned?

Those in the Action Capture the Learning

One option is to get the individuals and teams who are involved in the action to capture the learning. The after action review (AAR), a very useful tool, was developed by the U.S. Army for this purpose (Baird, Holland, and Deacon, 1999). The AAR is a structured process for a team to learn as they go. The AAR does not need to take long; thirty to forty-five minutes is usually all that is required. The point is to stop the action, learn quickly, and then apply what is learned back in the action. In business, people may want to take longer when the situation is complex or a lot is happening. Still, the objective is to capture lessons learned quickly and apply them so you can continue the learning and performing process (U.S. Army, 1993). The steps are fairly simple; in each step, you ask a single question:

Step 1: What was the intent?
Step 2: What happened?
Step 3: Based on our experience what have we learned?
Step 4: What do we do now?
Step 5: Whom do we tell about it?

In 1994, when the U.S. Army's 10th Mountain Division landed in Haiti during the peacekeeping efforts, the units used AARs as a process to quickly analyze and improve their performance. As would be expected, each unit began to learn and improve from its own perspective based on its own experiences. One unit located on the aircraft carrier *Eisenhower* discovered an immediate problem. The ship's hallways and stairs were designed for efficient and quick movement of navy personnel. Army personnel with eighty-pound packs could not easily go up and down the stairs, and it was impossible to pass each other in the hallways. The challenge was how to deploy three thousand troops quickly, even though one could not move effectively in the passageways. The solution developed was to use the large elevators, designed to raise the aircraft to the upper decks, to transport the troops and their gear.

Another unit discovered that it was very short on water. The soldiers' water consumption was much higher than expected because of the heat and humidity and so the need for potable water increased dramatically. This unit called for supply lines to be opened and the units responsible for supplying drinkable water to move up quickly. Yet another unit looked at its supply of intravenous equipment and projected a shortage. More soldiers than expected were fainting and needed IVs. They requested more medical supplies.

Solutions to all these problems offered valuable lessons at the local level that led to improved operational efficiency. But the next higher level was also doing AARs. By consolidating the information received from all of the units, those at this level gained a good overall picture of what was happening. They concluded that all three units described here had related issues. The soldier carrying eighty pounds of equipment in high temperature and humidity was losing too much body fluid. They suggested that the soldiers reduce what they carried to the bare essentials for a peacekeeping operation. This might reduce the physical exertion enough to prevent the soldiers from perspiring so heavily, and therefore minimize the need for so much extra water and IVs. One unit was directed to reduce its carrying load and see what happened; it was a success. The command went out to all units to minimize pack loads. Furthermore, the knowledge acquired during this campaign did not just have immediate effects; it was consolidated with lessons learned about water in Rwanda and Somalia to establish new recommendations for troops committed to peacekeeping operations. This knowledge was also put to use by the U.S. Army when it was called to help with the disaster relief effort organized in the wake of Hurricane Andrew in Florida.

AARs work because those involved in the action are most likely to capture knowledge that is useful to them. They produce *local value*—knowledge that can be used at the point of decision making (Sullivan and Harper, 1997). Those involved in helping to capture the lessons learned have to see results from their efforts—short-term, measurable, significant results on the job. If not, they will have little enthusiasm for the process. Tool 2 shows how BP has adapted the process to fit their needs.

Principle 3.3

To increase the likelihood of applicability and implementation, design knowledge capture to maximize local value.

Tool 2
THE AFTER ACTION REVIEW

WHAT IS AN AAR?

The after action review (AAR) is a simple process to help people learn from experience. AARs focus on learning during and immediately after an event so that people can apply what is learned as quickly as possible to subsequent actions. The ultimate objective is to improve performance. The process was developed by the U.S. Army to enable its transformation from a late "industrial age" army to an "information age" army for the twenty-first century. It is considered one of the most powerful learning tools ever used.

WHEN SHOULD YOU HAVE AN AAR?

The AAR is used during and immediately after each identifiable event while memory is fresh and unvarnished, participants are still available, and learning can be applied straightaway.

WHAT IS AN EVENT?

An event must have a beginning and an end. It may be either a small action or part of a larger action (shift handover, planning meeting, and so on).

HOW DO YOU CONDUCT AN AAR?

Every event is divided into specific activities, each of which should have an identifiable objective and plan of action. A discussion lasting thirty to forty-five minutes should cover each question.

What was supposed to happen? (Twenty-five percent of time is spent on this subject.) Everyone shares their understanding of what should have happened. It is established how well the objective and plan were understood from the start. Actions to correct any lack of clarity are identified.

What actually happened? (Twenty-five percent of time is spent on this subject.) The facts about what happened are established—the ground truth. In seeking the ground truth, the group tries to identify a problem, not a culprit.

Why were there differences? and *What can we learn?* (Fifty percent of time is spent on this subject.) The real learning begins when the group compares the plan to what actually happened. Successes and shortfalls are identified and discussed. Action plans are agreed on to sustain the successes and improve on the shortfalls.

WHO IS INVOLVED IN AN AAR?
Everyone involved in the event participates, including the team conducting the event and other teams that were involved. The leaders and participants are all on equal footing in the learning process. A facilitator (a team leader or a close observer of the project) ensures that everyone's views are heard but does not provide the answers.

IMPORTANT REMINDERS
It is important to be objective; balance inquiry and advocacy. There must be a climate of openness and learning; the objective is to fix the problem, not place blame. AARs are learning events, not evaluations or critique sessions.

Learnings must be converted into usable knowledge and disseminated to selected audiences for a broader learning experience throughout the organization. AARs can be audiotaped or videotaped for use as training tools, but conducting an AAR should never be put on hold because of unnecessary details. An AAR can be done with paper and pencil, and should be done at a key time during the event or as soon as possible afterward in order to capture the lessons learned while they are still fresh in participants' minds.

Source: Adapted from After Action Reviews, *by K. Pearse and G. Parcell.*

Someone Outside the Action Captures the Learning

Another option is to have someone outside the action capture the learning. These individuals can offer a new perspective and are more likely to be objective. Outside observers and evaluators who watch, either before or during the action, can validate and check what the people directly involved are finding. The disadvantage, of course, is that their conclusions are less likely to be accepted by the group because they are not directly involved. They have less direct knowledge on which to base their observations, but when used carefully, outsiders can provide valuable insights. There are two kinds of outside observers: learning observers assigned specifically to the unit, and peers.

Learning Observers

Learning observers may be assigned to specific units and given the responsibility of capturing the learning. Most often learning observers have expertise in the topic areas. For example, when the troops landed in Haiti learning observers were assigned in critical areas. These observers were drawn from the army's service schools based on their area of expertise. For example, Major Hughes, an expert in communications, was with the troops on the naval aircraft carrier *Eisenhower*. His assignment was not only to help coordination between the army and the navy but also to capture knowledge and feed it back to the army's Center for Lessons Learned. His observations were consolidated with those of others to develop the operating plans and doctrine to guide army and navy coordination in the future.

Learning observers can also be assigned during simulations and experiments. When General Sullivan was trying to determine the impact of the digitized battlefield in the Prairie Warrior simulation, he assigned observers to watch what happened and capture the learning. They focused on how the speed and accuracy of communications affected decisions and could mold processes. They focused on how to help commanders work with this new technology.

Tool 3
LEARNING OBSERVERS

WHAT IS A LEARNING OBSERVER?

A learning observer has a crucial part in an after action review (AAR). The observer assists the project manager by collecting data and providing feedback to the group participating in the project. As part of planning for an AAR, the project leader identifies both the observer and the person who will conduct the AAR; this may be the same person.

QUALIFICATIONS

Learning observers should be able to perform the tasks being taught, or have sufficient background and knowledge on the project area they will be observing. They should not have any responsibilities that would detract from their observer role. If personnel are not available to fulfill this role, then a senior manager should take it on. Learning observers and project leaders should be in sync about the methods and procedures to be used in order to ensure that feedback is relevant and appropriate.

RESPONSIBILITIES OF THE LEARNING OBSERVER

The project leader identifies the key points and critical events in the project on which to focus and to include in their evaluation. This ensures that the learning observer is present at these events and able to give the pertinent feedback necessary, because accessing every individual and action would obviously be impossible.

Reviews by Peers and Other External Subject Matter Experts

Others who do not participate in the action but can capture learning are peers and subject matter experts. Using a peer assist is simple: your peers look at what you are doing or planning to do and provide input. This is particularly valuable before an action is begun, but it can also be very useful during an action. Again, a few simple rules apply.

⇨ Be clear about the business problem or issue on which you are requesting help.

⇨ Provide as much up-front information as you can, so the peers helping you can spend their time focusing on offering suggestions.

⇨ Involve the peer group as early as possible. The sooner you have their suggestions, the more likely you will be able to include them in your processes.

⇨ Once you have heard from the peer group, be as specific as possible about what you can use and how. Telling the peer group what is useful will help them be better able to assist you in the future.

Subject matter experts not involved in the action can also add a valuable perspective. Their insights can validate and enhance what those involved in the action discover. However, their observations have to be seen as valid, useful, and meaningful by those doing the job. The experts have to understand that what they suggest is to be used to enhance performance and not for retribution or punishment for failure.

Principle 3.3

To increase validity, use learning observers, peers, or subject matter experts.

Tool 4
PEER ASSISTS

WHAT IS A PEER ASSIST?

A peer assist is a meeting or workshop where people from other business units share their experience, insights, and knowledge with a team that has requested help. A peer assist accomplishes the following:

➡ It targets a specific technical or commercial challenge.
➡ It gains assistance and insight from people outside the team and identifies possible approaches and new lines of inquiry.
➡ It promotes sharing of learning and develops strong networks among staff.

WHEN IS A PEER ASSIST APPROPRIATE?

A peer assist is appropriate when the cost of gathering the help is likely to result in significant benefits. It is appropriate when diverse views external to the business unit can broaden the range of options considered.

HOW DO YOU USE A PEER ASSIST?

Once a problem is defined, consider whether a peer assist is the most appropriate process to solve it. Write up the issues you face and identify the skills and experience that may help. Look for diversity in the people you ask to participate in the peer assist; even those with little direct experience can offer a great deal of insight. Identify a group that can meet for the period of time (up to a day) and specify who will facilitate the meeting. Set aside plenty of time for reflection and for analysis of findings. Once the key learning is captured, agree on a set of actions, and then disseminate the information to all parties involved and the whole organization.

NINE RULES FOR PEER ASSISTS

1. Plan the peer assist early to make use of the results in your business outcome. This is not just a step in the planning process; a peer assist is very effective in the planning and delivery stages as well.

2. Share your plans for a peer assist with others—they may have similar needs and can share the design.

3. Be clear in articulating the business problems or challenges you are asking the other group of peers to help you with. Be prepared to reframe these as you grapple with them in discussion with your peers. Give the team context by providing them with briefing material.

4. Assemble a group tailored to your objectives who have diverse skills and experience, people who will both challenge your mental models and offer options and new lines of inquiry. Consider inviting people from other disciplines, businesses, and companies.

5. The leader's role during the peer assist is to offer help, knowledge, and experience and to reduce the workload, not to criticize or add to the workload.

6. Plan your time so you can build the peer assist in early.

7. Prepare an action list at the end of the meeting. Monitor progress on the action list, and make sure the peers who have helped you know what you were able to accomplish.

8. Get each participant to consider what he or she has learned from the peer assist and will use afterward.

9. Consider who else might benefit from the lessons learned and share with them. Provide contact names for follow-up discussions.

Source: Adapted from Peer Assists, *by G. Parcell and N. Milton.*

Choices: Capturing Learning from Experience

When you *focus* you define the areas in which there is a knowledge gap. Now the question is which approach to take to acquire that knowledge. You have two choices. First, decide *who* will be responsible for capturing the lessons learned. Will it be someone involved in the action or someone outside of it? If the person is involved in the action, the tool to use is the after action review. If the person is outside of the action, the tools to use are learning observers and peer assists. Second, decide *when* the lesson will be captured. Will it be before or during the action? To capture the knowledge before the action takes place, a simulation or experiment must be designed. During-the-action knowledge capture requires that participants understand how to perform and learn at the same time. Figure 3.1 illustrates how the various strategies can be combined.

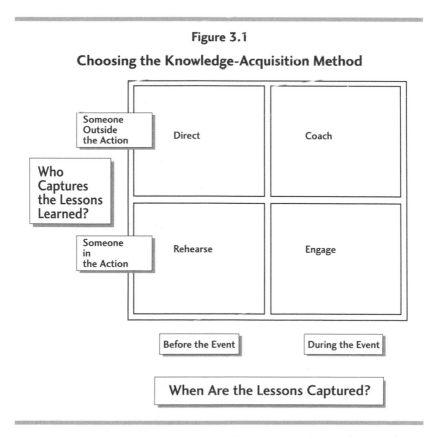

Figure 3.1

Choosing the Knowledge-Acquisition Method

In the Action/Before the Event:
Rehearse

Probably the most common way to capture learning before an event is a dress rehearsal. We are all familiar with the phase "practice makes perfect." By *rehearse* we mean the capability of those *involved* in the action to capture learning in a simulation.

Sainsbury's millennium Christmas rehearsal is an example of individuals and groups capturing the learning themselves before the event. Indeed, if designed correctly, a training event or simulation can be used to capture learning around defined topics, as well as to help participants learn how to do after action reviews to expand their skills in capturing learning during an event. At BP, before beginning work on a refinery turnaround—that is, totally refurbishing a refinery—participants are given a half-day session that includes role-plays and simulated construction exercises. They then use after action reviews to discover how to change their work processes and relationships before they get to the job. The advantage is that they not only save significant money by working out the kinks before beginning the job but also learn how to capture learning efficiently and quickly. When they get to the actual turnaround, what they have learned is a natural part of the work process.

In the Action/During the Event:
Engage

Involving those in the action to capture learning during an event is probably the most powerful way to drive improved performance. We use *engage* to describe actively involving those in the action in *real time* to analyze and learn from their experience. The after action review is the most frequently used tool for this. Not only the troops landing in Haiti knew how to do AARs—everyone in the U.S. Army is taught how and is expected to do them. AARs are so prevalent that popular writer Tom Clancy includes them in his novels, explaining how military action is done.

In their study of the Toyota production line, Spear and Bowen

(1999) provide another example of the power of learning during performance. At Toyota, workers all assume that their job is not only to do the actual tasks but to figure out ways to do them better. Every production unit has a job to get done as well as an experiment to run. This is successful when the people understand how to run the experiment and capture the learning. At Toyota each person knows what input they will receive into their job and what output they are responsible for. They are then given the latitude to test what happens to performance. They are constantly looking for improvement, and immediately pass on new knowledge to their supervisors.

Outside the Action/Before the Event:
Direct

The option that probably offers the most flexibility in trying new ideas and keeping very focused on a limited set of issues is a simulation with learning observers or peers involved. You can run what-if scenarios with observers watching to see what happens. This allows for learning before the real action, where the costs and consequences of what is done increase dramatically. It also allows the involvement of some real professionals or subject matter experts in capturing the learning.

They act as directors *observing* and guiding the action. By *direct* we mean the capability of an *external* person with the expertise necessary to observe and capture learning during a simulation. You can run what-if scenarios and target the knowledge-capturing efforts around specific topics. The army's Prairie Warrior simulation remains the best example. The observers or controllers who participate in the simulation are usually retired senior army officers who have a vast amount of experience to draw on to make sense of what they are seeing. They are also given very structured collection plans that focus them on the issues the commanders have designed into the exercise.

BP's peer assist is another good example. Before BP implements a plan, peers are invited to offer input. Peers not only add a new perspective but also themselves learn what others are doing correctly. They may find useful knowledge that they can transfer to their own operations.

Outside the Action/During the Event:
Coach

At some automobile firms, learning observers are assigned to product development teams. Each usually works with four to five teams. Their job is to observe what happens and consolidate learning around how to speed up the product development process. They have a very clear objective: cut the time it takes to get a car from idea to prototype to production. They have structured collection tools for that objective but also, like the learning observers assigned to units in the army, they are encouraged to watch carefully and capture anything that will help improve performance. They provide real-time feedback as well as capture lessons from across the organization. We use the term *coach* to summarize this sense of real-time learning. By coach we mean someone *on the field*, but not in the action, who has the expertise and access to capture lessons learned.

Some consulting firms adopt an interesting variation on this process. The learning observer they assign to one unit is a functioning member of another unit. These people have a twofold job. They capture the learning in the unit they are watching and help them apply it in their performance. Then they take what they learn back to their unit. Obviously, the people doing this job have to have great credibility in both units.

Expert advisers are also very useful in providing an external perspective. At Analog Devices, a company that develops signal processing equipment, expert advisers are brought in to review progress at each stage of a fixed product development process to capture lessons for both the team they are observing and higher-level management. They then consolidate what they learn across many teams in a quarterly report that is disseminated to all teams.

Which knowledge acquisition process should you choose? The answer depends on what you need to learn, how fast you need to learn it, and what level of risk you are willing to assume. When you choose when to capture learning you balance expense and risk on the one hand with applicability on the other. Capturing learning before events in a simulation is less risky and less expensive. People can recover from mistakes quickly. They can try out different scenarios to see which ones work. But the simulation must be realistic. When you capture learning during the event you gain applicability, but the expense and risk go up. Mistakes are costly and affect performance.

When you choose who captures the knowledge you must balance access and timeliness against a diverse perspective. If those in the action capture knowledge, they have immediate access to the lessons learned. They are, however, probably very biased. Those involved in the action usually take a very narrow and short-term perspective. It is hard to get a realistic view when the bullets are flying.

Principle 3.4

Choose the knowledge-capture process that maximizes the tradeoffs of risk and applicability against accessibility and bias.

Moving Forward

The organizational culture, processes, individual skills, and needs may require that one or more of these learning acquisition processes be used. If top management can clearly define an area where learning will have a significant impact and experts with experience in that area are available, then using learning observers in key units is probably the best idea. If the consequences of failure are high, then running a simulation before taking action is probably the best idea. If jobs can be defined so that customers, suppliers, and metrics of success are clear, then employees can probably be trained to perform and learn at the same time.

Structure

Pulling Knowledge into Performance

KNOWLEDGE HAS LITTLE VALUE unless it is used. Acquiring, cataloguing, and storing information merely offer potential; the value comes when the information is used. Information that sits in a repository because of formatting or timing problems or simple lack of motivation and is not used at the point of decision is worse than useless. Money and time have been spent to collect something that has no impact. Information must be consolidated and synthesized so people will want it and come and get it. They will thus pull the knowledge into their performance.

By *structure* we mean to validate, consolidate, and organize knowledge so that it is as attractive, usable, and accessible as possible. There are two questions to ask when choosing how to structure knowledge: *Why will they come? And how will they gain access?*

Why Will They Come?

It is not hard to imagine an organization creating a knowledge repository (Davenport and Prusak, 1998). A vision is established, a team formed, consultants and system integrators hired, and with hard work and good project management, six months or a year later, a knowledge repository is developed. Now, fast-forward to the one-year anniversary. A new project is in the incubation stage (linked to the Internet, no doubt). But the knowledge base has not been updated, and it is simply yesterday's news and of very little value for the new initiative.

Benefits accrue from a knowledge base if a firm effectively builds on the early investments and continues to improve both the content and the process for acquiring that content. Benefits continue to accrue if the content in the repository is perceived as relevant, timely, and valid. If not, then the knowledge initiative will, like a shooting star, burn brightly for a moment but quickly fade before there is any real change or impact on performance. Knowledge sharing is a journey, not an event, and the firm must have a strategy to ensure that carefully acquired and effectively organized information will be updated and available now and in the future. It is essential to have a clear strategy for the care and feeding of the knowledge base so that it is useful and used. We call this strategy the *administrative strategy*.

Our research suggests two basic approaches to developing an administrative strategy for the knowledge base, and each has its strengths and weaknesses. At one end of the administrative continuum, a *focal unit* is given responsibility to structure knowledge. A focal unit is a designated group of individuals (often cross-functional) who are given accountability for creating and sustaining knowledge initiatives over time. People will then come and use the knowledge because they accept the expertise or power of those individuals in structuring the decision. At the other end of the administrative continuum, a *community* is responsible for structuring the knowledge. This community of individuals has a common purpose and relies on one another to solve shared problems. People are quick to accept those things they have a part in creating and understand because of their involvement. For example, sales representatives readily adapt the techniques of their peer groups and service technicians quickly access knowledge about products and services presented in a format they helped create. U.S. Army personnel use the knowledge that comes from their own after action reviews, which are organized in a structure they developed.

Focal units and communities both work. Neither is inherently better, but they are different from each other. Failure to recognize the differences can result in a governance structure that will confuse and undermine the firm's ability to sustain its efforts around any knowledge-sharing initiative.

Focal Units

A focal unit may be given the responsibility to define the scope of the initiative, understand the processes used to acquire and validate knowledge assets, and structure what is captured to make it useful. This group does not need to be centralized corporate staff. It can be a group in a business unit. It may even simply be one individual who is seen to be qualified for the job because of expertise or position. When a focal unit is a team, it often works best if it is cross-functional, thus avoiding an emphasis on any one functional perspective, such as technology.

Focal units are used by some of the top organizations we work with. Xerox has tiger teams. The U.S. Army has the Center for Army Lessons Learned. BP's knowledge management group is similar, and Lucent Technologies has an organization effectiveness group.

There are obvious advantages to giving one unit responsibility for a knowledge initiative. The group can quickly and consistently form a shared vision and approach. What is known can be rapidly driven into consistent standards and methods. As long as their authority is accepted, they can quickly scale up their efforts applying them in other areas and to much bigger projects. Leadership and accountability for implementation are clear. The group can control and focus what is available and reach the general population both in and out of the organization. A focal unit can also maintain control over intellectual property. For example, a bank may want to control the structure and content of its new strategy. Similarly, a pharmaceutical firm legally has to control what information on new products it shares with doctors, hospitals, and patients until it receives approval from the Food and Drug Administration. A focal unit need not be centralized. But if it is decentralized, the team must understand the performance criteria, the work process, and how the knowledge will be used.

When responsibility is given to one group, one very large issue arises: how to gain acceptance throughout the organization. The group may not have the organizational power or be perceived as having the expertise to drive use and implementation. Even if the group is successful at creating the assets, it runs the risk of failing to motivate others to use them. In this case, once again, time and money will be spent generating knowledge that no one uses.

Principle 4.1

Use a focal unit to structure knowledge when: (1) the performance objective requires rapid scaling; (2) issues of risk and intellectual property require control; and (3) recognized expertise will be helpful.

Communities

The second administrative strategy is to use a community of purpose to structure knowledge (Storck and Hill, 2000). In its purest sense, a community is a loosely linked group that shares a purpose and through ongoing interactions helps achieve the objectives of the individuals in the group. The individuals draw from and feed into the collective experience. Leadership in a community is very different from in a focal unit and is usually not connected to a hierarchical leadership structure. A community is the best option for structuring the knowledge when:

⇨   The knowledge is context-specific and difficult to codify.
⇨   When creativity and innovation are needed to make sense of diverse experience and information.

⇨ When knowledge is scattered throughout a large heterogeneous group.

⇨ When sustained commitment from a large group of people is needed over a long period of time.

In 1997 Xerox needed to totally revamp its information architecture to standardize around common purposes (Storck and Hill, 2000). The information technology groups scattered throughout the organization had, over the years, adopted their own specific architecture based on the particular needs of the business units they served. This was good for the business units but made it difficult to share information across units effectively, and more importantly, to adapt to change quickly. In the past, faced with comparable problems, Xerox had relied on a centralized staff group to set standards and define processes for structuring and sharing information. Experience had shown, however, that these standards eroded over time as each decentralized group, under the pressure to serve its particular business unit, simply customized and created its own structure.

To establish the new communication platform, Xerox created what it called the Transition Alliance. The information technology community was brought together, given the problem of creating a coherent architecture, and asked to implement it. As the group worked together, diverse viewpoints were consolidated, differences were ironed out, and eventually common approaches emerged. When they emerged, they were understood and supported by all. More important, over time the Transition Alliance became the monitoring group, using peer pressure to get continued compliance and make modifications as necessary.

Individuals often develop a strong sense of identity with their respective communities. In fact, one of the risks an organization runs when it fosters and helps establish communities of purpose is that the people become so strongly identified with their peer groups that they lose sight of the purpose of the overall organization. This often occurs in highly specialized fields such as engineering, medicine, and education. For example, one organization we studied decided to change the programming languages it used for all new product development. The decision met with fierce resistance from a well-formed community committed to the existing language. The engineer and program manager argued passionately for their views. Eventually, the firm had to disband the organizational unit in which the main part of the community resided—a long, difficult, and costly process. Yet this same group's passion had previously been the source of extremely high productivity.

A community is much better at monitoring itself over an extended period of time and in gaining acceptance for what they decide than a smaller group (such as a focal unit) that must motivate the rest of the organization. However, the community will also be slower and less likely to match a predefined set of criteria. If a community is used, then the organization will have to spend a considerable amount of time supporting and sustaining them so they can get their work done.

Principle 4.2

Use a community to structure knowledge when (1) experience and knowledge are highly dispersed; (2) knowledge is very context-specific and hard to codify; and (3) commitment from a large group is needed over an extended period of time.

In sum, structuring knowledge takes a good understanding of the nature of the work processes, how the knowledge will be used, and how best to get people to use it.

How Will They Gain Access?

Knowledge assets do no good unless those responsible for performance can gain access to them. From the perspective of the individual who needs the information, the difficulty lies in making sense of all the available information. How do they find, retrieve, and assimilate knowledge, and then turn it into action and performance? Two factors influence this process: the way an individual thinks and uses information, and the nature of the information itself.

Each person interprets a given piece of knowledge in a unique way, influenced both by his or her own personal traits and how he or she understands the current work or problem issues (Weick, 1995). Consider, for example, the difference between how a novice and an expert might interpret the same lesson. With little or no experience and poorly formed mental models, the novice looks for concrete facts, often applying a process or procedure in cookbook fashion. For example, at Xerox new service agents are very careful to follow what is in their manual. The experts, on the other hand, read between the lines, adapting or refining the materials based on their own experience and their own way of collecting information.

An organization can try to influence the way people see and interpret information by framing it in a particular way. An *active frame* sifts and sorts the information so people can see it in an organizational format. Searching is simplified and efficient because the categories have a concept or meaning. The focus is on providing usable information in defined categories in an efficient format. A *passive frame* does some preliminary sorting, but basically presents the information as is and lets the user try to make sense of it. Searching is more of a discovery process; the person makes sense by weaving together many sources and points of data. The searcher constructs or finds meaningful information or knowledge.

Efficiency: The Active Frame

Examples of active frames abound in organizations, but benchmarking is probably the best example. People engage in benchmarking with specific questions to be answered and categories to be investigated. The frame used for collection limits the information collected. The results of the benchmarking study are then structured carefully, usually in relation to the process being studied. For example, when automobile firms carried out benchmarking studies on lean manufacturing, team members knew what they were looking for. The search and the information gathered were most often organized in terms of the stages of their own production process. This active frame enabled U.S. automobile executives to avoid wasting time looking at irrelevant activities.

The potential knowledge consumer who is accessing information is therefore guided through results and conclusions by the frame imposed. Findings are organized and presented in a manner that make it easy to find and use them. When there is sufficient clarity in the performance process, when the steps and sequence are known, then it is a good idea to structure knowledge so people can find what they need quickly and efficiently. An active frame that structures and organizes the information minimizes cost and search time. And there lies both the greatest strength and greatest weakness of the active frame.

For example, in the automobile case, the initial frames were the firm's own production process. Based on that the effort required to access the knowledge was reduced. Everything was organized according to the way in which their employees were already conditioned to work. A limited set of knowledge fit within the performance structure. When a team went on a benchmarking trip to Toyota, it already had categories of information in place and was able to use them to guide its search. As the team gathered information the frame became easier to understand, codify, and use, because it could be related to the phases. However, the groups often missed the fact that Toyota's system relied on much more integrated and overlapping phases, which are as much or more important than what happens throughout a given production phase. The groups also failed to realize that each person at Toyota had the mandate and capability to learn and improve his or her own portion of the process. The processes and techniques of constant change and improvement at the individual level, as well as how they are aggregated to overall product development levels, were far more important than the phases themselves. Thus, although the frames U.S. executives used allowed their benchmarking teams to focus on improving phases, they did not help them question the overlaps or show how to totally redesign their own development process if necessary. In sum, active frames make the collection and interpretation process easier, but they often limit the perspective and conclusions.

Novices in particular can be led astray by an active frame. On the one hand they are greatly helped because an active frame guides their activities. On the other hand, they are more likely to believe what they see or read, rather than interpret it based on their experience, ask the hard questions, or capture what is important and ignore the rest. Of course, if the knowledge they gain is relevant, that is not a bad thing. But if the frame leads novices down the wrong path, they have no way of knowing they are headed in the wrong direction.

Generally speaking, when what needs to be accomplished and the areas where knowledge is needed are defined, either because top management has defined them or because the work processes are so clear that they define the criteria themselves, then the active frame for knowledge is appropriate.

Active Framing: Process Maps

Process mapping is an example of active framing. When we go on a major trip, we usually spend the necessary time preparing. We plan ahead and take the necessary precautions, such as making sure that our equipment functions properly, deciding and preparing what will be necessary or helpful for our journey, and most importantly, getting maps that will lead us to our destination. We follow a sequence of activities. Drawing maps detailing these activities allows us not only to plan the trip more efficiently but also to add new knowledge at each step along the way.

A map is a chart or graph that depicts the relationship of the variables that are significant to the project. Drawing a map forces you to consolidate and integrate information and develop usable knowledge of the process (Hayes, Wheelwright, and Clark, 1988). Tool 5 shows how to map the product development process. In this case, it is shaped like a funnel. The wide mouth of the funnel makes it easy to catch new ideas and product concepts, but the funnel narrows as people start making choices about what is feasible. As the product moves forward it passes various stages where decisions are made about what goes forward and how.

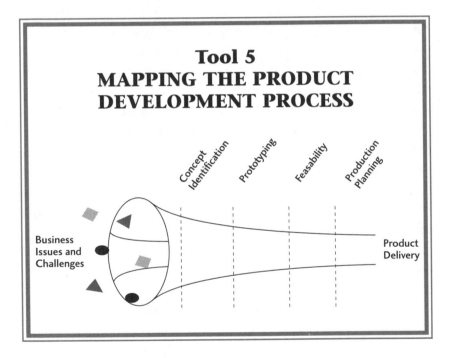

Tool 5
MAPPING THE PRODUCT DEVELOPMENT PROCESS

Concept Identification

Prototyping

Feasibility

Production Planning

Business Issues and Challenges

Product Delivery

The phases and gates provide a way to map out the product development process and can serve as the structure for the knowledge-capture process. Each phase ends and begins with a gate, where it is natural to ask what has been learned. This knowledge is captured and stored. The next group of product ideas coming through the gate then has the advantage of building on what has been learned from previous products.

No matter what process you focus on, it can be mapped out and the key decision points identified. Knowledge can then be captured and consolidated around those decision points. Process mapping becomes a way to actively structure knowledge that fits the work flow.

Principle 4.3

Use an active frame when: (1) you know the nature and sequence of the performance process; (2) the scope of knowledge needed is narrow and can be limited by the nature of the performance process; and (3) you need efficiency in implementation.

Searching: The Passive Frame

The passive frame is the opposite approach. A passive frame provides some general guidance but does not greatly limit what is gathered or how it is sorted. The exact nature of the performance process is not known; creativity is needed. A classic example of a passive frame is the library's Dewey Decimal System. This system organizes an extremely diverse knowledge base into broad manageable categories. When you go to the library, you may have a general or specific idea of what you are looking for and the Dewey Decimal System helps you find it either by providing you with the specific number associated with the book or by allowing you to look through categories. But you must know what you are looking for before you can search out the possibilities.

The term most often used to describe such an approach today is *metadata*. Metadata is the broad organizing structure for a knowledge base. It is essentially data about data. Within this broad frame, data mining, search engines, and Web technologies allow people to find nuggets of insight among the millions of pages of information in cyberspace. With these techniques and tools, the frame becomes even more passive.

When you cannot predict what people will need to know, when you are not sure about what will lead to good performance, and when people will need to be creative, then a passive frame is appropriate. The focus will shift from actively structuring the information to providing access through search capability.

Passive Framing:
The Search Engine

For examples of passive framing, look at the home page of the Center for Army Lessons Learned (**http://call.army.mil/**). This is the repository for information on what is learned and done in military action. Figure 4.1 shows CALL's home page.

Notice how extensive the material is. They even have a search engine for search engines. The assumption is that users will define what they are looking for, and if they don't, will discover it in the search process. No frame is forced on users because their needs are unpredictable. Without any structure to the search process users are on their own. But often the gold is in the search, not in the find. With no forced frame of reference, users are free to explore. As they search, they make associations where none existed before, test out wild ideas, and go down unexplored paths. They are in control and are more likely to explore a wide range of issues, develop new ways of thinking, and form unique answers to their questions.

When performance criteria are not clear—either because the situation is ambiguous or it is best for people to discover on their own how to perform better—their search should not be limited by an active frame. Rather, they should be aided in the search processes. The knowledge base should be structured so that it is easy for them to go from one idea to the other, to understand linkages and flows, but also so that their creativity is not limited.

Figure 4.1

Home Page of the Center for Army Lessons Learned

 Dogpile Search Site
Searches multiple sites

 SemioMap Visual Search
Searches CALL products
and other selected military
sites

 Northen Light Search
Searches Internet plus
a special collection of
one million articles

 **MetaCrawler
Search Site**
Searches multiple sites

 ProQuest Direct
Searches for information
in thousands of different
journals, periodicals, dissertations, news-
papers, and magazines.
*Available only to individuals accessing from Fort
Leavenworth or registered CALL DB users*

Other Search Engines
Links to other search
engines

Other Search Engines

Federal Web Locator	**Government Information Locator**
Army Search	**Navy Search**
Air Force Link Search	**MarineLink**
Army Doctrine and Training Digital Library	**DefenseLINK**
AccuFind	GoTo.com
ALIWEB	HotBot
All-In-One Search Page	Inter-Links Internet Access
AltaVista	Infoseek
AOL Search	Infohiway Inc.
Ask Jeeves	LookSmart
CARRIE: A Full Text Electronic Library	Lycos
C4 TotalSearch Technology	Magellan Internet Guide
C/Net Share.com	MetaCrawler Search Site
DejaNews	MSN Search
Direct Hit	Netscape Search
Electric Library	Reference.com (Usenet & Listserve)
Excite	SavvySearch
Fast Search	The BigHub.com
Galaxy: The Professionals Guide	Whois.net (domain information)
to a World of Information	WhoWhere?
	Yahoo

Principle 4.4

Use a passive frame when: (1) the structure of the work process is not known; (2) the scope of the knowledge needed is broad and cannot be limited by the nature of the performance process; and (3) creativity is needed.

Choices: Structuring Knowledge So People Will Come

By combining the two dimensions—administrative strategy and sense-making method—we create four prototype knowledge-structuring processes. None of them is any better or worse; each has strengths and weaknesses. The one you choose will depend on the specific context of your knowledge initiative. The objective is to increase the probability that people will come and use the knowledge assets you have created. Figure 4.2 illustrates how the various strategies can be combined.

Passive Frame/Focal Unit:
Mining

The Center for Army Lessons Learned is arguably one of the largest repositories of knowledge. The focal unit is located at Fort Leavenworth, Kansas. The chief of staff has given it the charge to collect, consolidate, and validate lessons learned from around the world and to define the nature and structure of the repository. The knowledge base includes not only high-level summaries but also detailed operations orders. The army does not provide an active frame. One commander's challenges may be quite different from another's. Searchers have to go into the knowledge base, consolidate what they need, and move it to action. The army does provide extensive search engines to help users comb through the massive amounts of

Figure 4.2

Choosing the Knowledge-Structuring Strategy

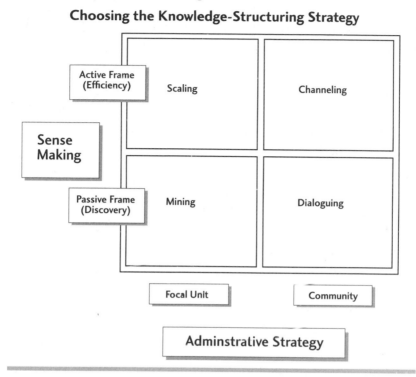

information available: a passive frame. The focal unit organizes the knowledge assets so others can mine the knowledge. By *mining* we mean the capability to *search and retrieve* knowledge assets from a large, diverse knowledge base

When Hurricane Andrew hit Florida in 1992 the army was deployed to assist in securing vital areas and in the cleanup. The colonel who received the assignment in the middle of the night knew very little about hurricanes or disaster relief. All he knew was that he had to get the troops out of bed and into action quickly. Before he roused the troops he clicked on the home page of the Center for Army Lessons Learned and started to search using keywords such as *hurricanes, disaster, Red Cross,* and *emergency preparedness.* He quickly found the agencies with which he needed to coordinate. He found operations orders others had used in emergency situations that he could quickly modify and dispatch. He also found that a water supply was critical. He began searching for knowledge on water purification. He found help in an unlikely place: Bosnia. The troops going into Bosnia had needed potable water; the contaminated water available there would make them and the rest of the population sick. In this area he found not only directions but implementation plans, lessons learned, and recommendations for dealing with contaminated water. Because he could search quickly he found what he needed and the troops were in the field quickly with knowledge that helped them save property and lives.

Passive Frame/Community:
Dialoguing

Passive frames create dialogue opportunities in a community. Dialogue creates the structure. By *dialoguing* we mean the capability of a community to evolve a knowledge structure through a high degree of *interaction*. For example, years ago, if people were interested in tracing their roots, they probably would have done a lot of trudging through old graveyards and flipping through musty old books. The Church of Jesus Christ of Latter-day Saints, however, has long been interested in genealogy. They have been copying and microfilming everything they could find for a very long time, storing it in a big granite mountain in Utah. In the 1970s they began to computerize all this information, unifying all the family trees that had already been linked together. Because of the computerization, information originally available only on microfiche was made available on computer disks, and now is found on CD-ROMs and the Internet. So if someone today was interested in finding out whom my great grandfather's sister married and where she lived, he could just go searching. As long as he knew her name, birth date, and place of birth, and as long as someone else had already bumped into her during their own search and taken the time to submit the records, he could find her. In order to do the sorting and storing, the church bought a large bank of Cray computers and now has the largest genealogical collection in the world. Stop in and see if you can find yourself, your grandparents, or better yet your great-great-great-great-grandparents. You might find someone you would be fascinated to know . . . or someone you would rather not know. Next, the Church is augmenting what is currently available by making all of its records accessible through the Web. It is up and running at **www.familysearch.org**.

This is an example of a great source that depends on the user's knowledge of what he is looking for and his ability to find work already done by someone else. The dialogue across many users linking fathers and mothers to sons and daughters creates an evolving structure that makes it easier and easier to find descendants. Without it, he would have to get in a car, drive across country, and spend the time and money searching around the old cemetery himself.

Since the development of the World Wide Web, life has become even easier for the genealogist. Another example of current genealogy efforts and where they are headed is the World Genealogy Web Project (**www.worldgenweb.org**). Founded in 1996 by Dale Schneider, the project attempts to link users, both professionals and beginners, to the information they are searching for. It has set up regional home pages throughout the world that are maintained by volunteers and genealogists who live in those regions. The information found at the various Web sites is supplied almost entirely by their users, and the Web sites themselves are linked in an intricate network that grows based on searches and additions of records.

Here's how it works. While researching a particular line of ancestors, a genealogist may come across scores of vital statistics that, while not immediately valuable to her own specific needs, could be extremely valuable to others. She posts those vital statistics on the World Genealogy Web Project's regional Web site for the corresponding region. That information is then available to other users of the Web site who may be searching for that specific information.

The project also has a valuable query feature. Records of ancestors, including birth dates, death dates, marriage dates, and parents' names, are often included in church records, town census records, and other historical sources. But those sources are kept in the libraries and churches of the town they come from. In order to get that information, genealogists formerly had to travel to the towns. This becomes an even greater problem when one's ancestors were immigrants and the records reside in foreign countries. With the query feature of the World Genealogical Web Project, a person can identify the town or community that holds the records and make a query to the appropriate regional Web site. A genealogist there, who does have physical access to the desired information, will go and do the research and simply pass it along. All this is done voluntarily, with the understanding that those who submit requests may have similar requests submitted to them. They then might have to do the legwork to find another's information in their region. Overall, those involved have been very excited about their findings and the ease with which they can search.

Although all participants have different goals, they understand that they share a greater goal, and that by sharing information with each other they may also gain better access to their own desired information. The frame around the information emerges over time. The network grows based on the interest and success of various members, and there is no centralized coordination, much less many rules. The idea is simply to search, have fun, link families together, and share and help out someone else if you wish. The community search drives the growth of the repository. A lot of the magic in this approach to genealogy is that when a person simply helps himself and adds to his own data, he is adding to what is available to everyone else, and the sites grow continuously.

Active Frame/Focal Unit:
Scaling

Xerox Corporation leveraged its strong community structure in quite a different way. Early fieldwork at Xerox PARC revealed that service technicians often shared knowledge in the form of tips (Stork and Hill, 2000). An experienced technician would help another with a difficult service problem based on how he or she had repaired a machine in a similar context. A tip might be, "Be sure to look to see if the air conditioner vent is directing air onto the paper feeder—that always seems to cause problems with that model." Xerox's challenge was to leverage this inefficient way of sharing knowledge. The company needed to scale up this concept so it could affect a service force of twenty thousand people located around the world. They needed to scale their learning. By *scaling* we mean aggregating, validating, and then *imposing a frame* that allows widespread and consistent knowledge sharing.

Xerox's Eureka Project is the initiative the company designed to scale knowledge from one service technician to many others. Any technician discovering a better way can submit his or her "tip" to a tiger team—a team that includes experts in each machine area, where the tips are validated and tested. The validation group is responsible for working with field agents to make sure the tips submitted are as accurate and complete as possible. Then they make an assessment of those that will have the biggest impact, combine tips to remove redundancy, delete tips that are no longer useful or have been superseded, and ensure quality before sending the tips on to the larger community. Validated tips are consolidated by equipment category and structured in a decision tree format—that is, if this is the problem check here and test for A and B; if B is the problem look for C and D; if you find C do this. Each tip is "published" with supporting examples, drawings, and its author's name. The structured data are made available to the rest of the field staff through an online information system and service agents access it when they hit a problem and are looking for ways others have solved comparable problems. The decision tree structure allows them to quickly search and pinpoint relevant knowledge.

The online system also allows individuals to track the status of their tips, when and how they are validated, and how they are used. Eventually, tips are analyzed to identify product modification, which will make servicing easier and provide the specifications for new products. The knowledge asset is structured in such a way that it fits directly into the ongoing work processes, developed and validated by those who, either because of experience or position, are viewed as experts. People are motivated to access and use the knowledge because it improves their performance. The Eureka Project's structure not only reinforces concepts and procedures acquired during formal training but also enables all individuals to contribute to the firm's performance in a clear and efficient manner. When Xerox deployed this approach, it achieved significant improvements—15 percent to 20 percent productivity increases. (See Figure 4.3 on page 83.)

We offer the Eureka solution as an example of the focal unit/active frame model for two reasons. First, a core group at Xerox works to keep the overall process effective. Although peer assists and the tip sources are community-based, decisions about format, structure, and ultimately scope of the knowledge base are made centrally. In part, this is a function of scale efficiencies. It takes a dedicated group to keep the system current and accurate. It cannot be sustained well by a voluntary team. Furthermore, content validation is critical. Bad ideas have to be weeded out. A focal unit can ensure this kind of quality control. It is interesting that both BP and Xerox leverage a strong community base. Their strategies for leveraging, however, are quite different.

Principle 4.5

To increase use of knowledge assets choose a structure that matches the organization's work process and performance requirements.

Active Frame/Community: Channeling

BP has many rigs in the water at any given time drilling for oil. As would be expected in such complex environments, problems arise and learning is constant. How do you adapt if the supplies do not arrive when you need them? What is the best course of action if you hit a new type of rock formation? Any number of problems may occur while drilling, but when the professionals on the rigs started talking together they discovered that many of the problems were common. Often the creative solution found to unstick a pipe in one area could be used or adapted by a drilling team in another area. If drill engineers could develop some mechanisms for sharing across platforms, they would save the time they spent inventing solutions for problems that had already been solved.

BP launched the Drilling Learning Project (already mentioned in Chapter 2) to facilitate this kind of knowledge-sharing. Community members were brought together and given the task of improving the knowledge-sharing effectiveness of the community—improving because knowledge sharing was already happening in the community. People met, asked for help, and attended conferences to share best practices and many other formal and informal ways of exchanging knowledge. In fact, they acted much like the genealogy community described in the previous section.

The Drilling Learning Project initiative, however, had a specific goal: for the community to put into place a knowledge structure that would channel the exchange into critical areas, thus driving efficiency and having a demonstrable performance impact. In effect, BP wanted to put in place an active frame to aid the knowledge-sharing process. The group, with feedback from the larger community, conducted a process to identify key performance categories that drove performance and for which a base of knowledge existed. They then selected a subset of these categories and developed a common frame for connecting knowledge assets related to each. By *channeling* we mean the capability of a *community to construct a common frame* that focuses knowledge assets in key areas.

Each category was assigned to a specific community member who had responsibility to facilitate the identification of key learnings, consolidate them, and make them available to the rest of the community through a Web site for a key category. They organized the site into three levels: principles, generic processes, and local

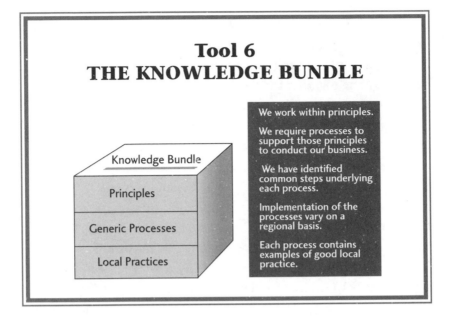

Tool 6
THE KNOWLEDGE BUNDLE

Knowledge Bundle

Principles

Generic Processes

Local Practices

We work within principles.

We require processes to support those principles to conduct our business.

We have identified common steps underlying each process.

Implementation of the processes vary on a regional basis.

Each process contains examples of good local practice.

practice. Local practice is how knowledge is applied and controlled by the contributing members of the community. The generic process is the road map that provides the active frame. The principles provide a means for the community to enforce shared values, beliefs, and assumptions. Tool 6 provides an example of a knowledge bundle: by combining knowledge about principles, processes, and practices, a full picture of an area is developed.

Moving Forward

The structure for the knowledge base is determined by what your organization needs to accomplish. It is the leader's responsibility and opportunity to make this choice. The worst mistake is to assume that if the knowledge is collected, then people will access and use it. This process of creating knowledge assets is a bit like making sausages. You may not be real sure what is in there, but when you turn the crank, good things come out. For those of us who do not do it intuitively, we need a little help to consolidate, eliminate, and make sense of what we have. The tools and exam-

Figure 4.3

Xerox's Eureka Project

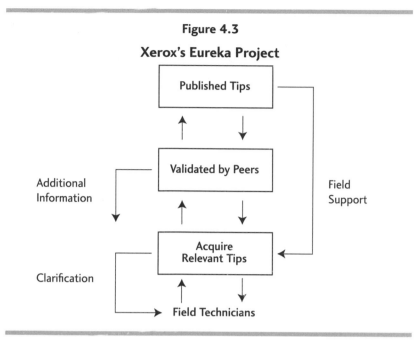

ples we have presented are not intended to be exhaustive. Statistics and strategic analysis are all about turning data into knowledge and provide a myriad of excellent tools. Use the ones that work for you. The leader's responsibility is to create a knowledge base that is so compelling and applicable that people will use it. They will constantly be pulling what is learned into their daily work and driving their own performance.

Target

Pushing Knowledge into Performance

As WE HAVE ALREADY STATED, all efforts to create knowledge assets are for naught unless those who need them come, get them, and use them. But sometimes they just will not come. The ancient Chinese philosopher who said, "When the learner is ready, the teacher should appear" was only partially right. The knowledge you have collected may well be too crucial to hold until learners discover that they need it and that it is available. Sometimes you have to deliver the knowledge to them. But it does no good to show financial data to doctors who neither understand nor have any way of interpreting and using the information. Or to provide clinical trial data to the pharmacist whose whole orientation is to fill prescriptions. Or, similarly, to provide market knowledge to a product development group after a competitive group has already launched a similar product.

When you *target* the knowledge base you are employing a push strategy. As we saw in the last chapter, a pull strategy assumes that users will know what they want, search until they find it, and then pull it into use. The knowledge simply has to be made available to them in a format that facilitates their search process. In contrast, by *target* we mean identifying specific consumers and designing and packaging the information so that it meets their needs and then aggressively making it available. Targeting prescreens potential knowledge assets, selects only what the user would view as relevant, and then pushes it into performance.

Merck and Company, Inc. provides an example. Merck's corporate culture is centered on knowledge. The corporation has been built on its ability to develop and bring to market pharmaceutical products that enhance the lives of people the company serves. In the marketplace the company capitalizes on its research capability by striving to stay ahead of the competition by launching new products and being first to market. In a typical scenario, a new product is developed using the company's internal research capability and knowledge about the new products; its indications and usage are disseminated to the market through professional channels; and sales come as a result of the superiority of the new product.

In the new economy, competitors not only have more ways to find out what is being developed within other corporations but also have the capability to leverage the general knowledge developed by Merck and increase the sales of their own, comparable products. In many areas, Merck has lost market share as a result. Merck has realized that its success in the future will be determined not only by its research capability but also by how well it can target the knowledge it creates to the right audience at the right time.

Merck's successful experience with its drug, Zocor, is a recent example of this new strategy. Zocor reduces the lipid level in the blood, decreasing the bad cholesterol and increasing the good cholesterol level. Multiple clinical trials conducted by the National Institutes of Health demonstrated that appropriate and consistent use of Zocor, and comparable drugs, extended the life of cardiac patients. The benefits of the treatment were also detailed in scholarly journals and in presentations at professional meetings. But the knowledge was having little impact. History was repeating itself. Aspirin and later beta-blockers had also both been proven effective in aiding cardiac patients but had followed the same lengthy adoption curve as the knowledge gradually spread among the medical community. Six years after launch, only 30 percent of those who could have been helped by these drugs were being prescribed the medication; after sixteen years on average only 50 percent were, and after twenty years only 80 percent of doctors were prescribing these drugs that had been proven to save lives. The challenge was obvious: how to get the right knowledge to the right place in the right format to reduce the length of the adoption cycle.

Based on its understanding of the industry, the adoption cycle, and the patient payoff, Merck set three objectives for its targeting efforts with Zocor (Griffin, 1999). First, it wanted to decrease the lengthy adoption cycle. Second, it wanted to grow the market for this category of drug through education of the stakeholders. Third, it wanted to increase its own share of the expanding market.

To accomplish these goals, Merck focused on key knowledge gaps. It needed to get the right type of data—patient care and financial data—to doctors and HMO administrators who would actually value the information. Merck sponsored the Scandinavian Symbostat Survival Study (Lancet, 1994), which determined the financial implications of repeat cardiac visits to the HMOs. This study provided financial and patient data, based on cardiac patients over a wide population. This was the kind of data that doctors and administrators would understand and believe.

Merck also analyzed the typical diagnosis process for cardiac patients—from initial visit with a primary care physician to visits with the hospital's cardiologist—to identify the type and form of information that was used. With this study, Merck located a disconnect between the primary care physician and the hospital. There was no feedback, neither the hospitals nor the doctors knew what happened to patients after they left the hospital—that is, their state of health, the progress they were making, or even whether they survived—unless the patients returned as a result of another cardiac event. The right process was not in place to push the right information to the right people at the right time. Consequently, doctors would often see patients on repeat visits only after it was either too late or very expensive to intervene in a way that would have any impact. Because of their focus, these information customers were not coming to get the information that would help them.

Merck recognized that doctors were much more likely to listen to and use information they received from opinion leaders and other respected doctors than from a pharmaceutical firm. Working with the opinion leaders at the hospital and with university academics, it helped to establish the Heart Care Network (Griffin, 1999). The Heart Care Network in select HMOs tracked the flow of patients into, out of, and back to hospitals. Rather than solely focus on expert knowledge from clinical trials as had been done in the past, the network provided process knowledge that was pushed to the doctors so they would be able to track their patients' compliance and progress. For example, Merck paid hospital staff to follow up on the health of patients and track their medication record one month, three months, and six months after being released from hospital. If patients were lax about taking their medication, the information was passed on to the doctors. That simple piece of information given to the doctors at the critical time, before a second cardiac event, saved lives.

Thus, Merck did not wait for the doctors to come searching. Instead, it made sure to deliver the right information to the right users at the right time in the right format. The partnership between Merck, the decision makers, and the opinion leaders in doing this resulted in a win-win-win situation. The patients' quality of life improved as the death rate from cardiac disease was reduced and their health management improved. The physicians gained professionally because they were better able to care for and diagnose their patients. The HMOs reduced their costs, while also learning about their own processes and how to improve service. Finally, Merck increased sales of Zocor from under $1 billion to more than $3 billion in eighteen months while also shortening the drug's adoption cycle.

Microsegmenting

If we are to deliver knowledge when and where it is needed we have to know a lot about the consumers of that knowledge. In the world of marketing, one of the most dramatic advances made possible by information technology is *microsegmentation* (Peppers and Rogers, 1999). Often also described as mass customization or one-on-one marketing, the concept is to customize the product or service to the point that each segment has only one customer (Pine, 1999). Hence, the ultimate effort is mass customization on the order of one. In order to mass-customize to this extent, the firm needs to develop two capabilities.

First, the firm must be able to define and continuously update the characteristics and *preferences* of customers. Customers' demands are always changing and evolving. If a company is going to respond to their needs, it has to know how they are changing. This alone creates an enormous need for information about the customers. Furthermore, customers do not only change their preferences, they also learn. If a company is good at providing them the right knowledge at the right time, they will eventually want new knowledge in different forms. To be responsive, companies need continuous interaction and dialogue with their customers to create a mutual learning process. The customers use the knowledge the company provides to improve their performance and capability. The company uses its understanding of their changing needs to update and improve its knowledge. Knowledge leads to performance, and performance leads back to knowledge.

Second, a company needs to be able to *package* knowledge quickly so that it meets the customers' needs. This is what Haeckel (1999) is referring to when he talks about the ability to understand—to sense and respond to—what the customer wants, package the right goods and services, and deliver quickly. Organizations need not only a superb marketing capability but also the ability to produce products and services in the time frame customers require. Flexible manufacturing technologies replace rigid, long-networked production lines. Modular, adaptive processes replace fixed production lines in order to give firms this type of flexibility (Baldwin and Clark, 1997). As such technologies that involve higher levels of information emerge, manufacturers get closer and closer to their objective of lot sizes of one. Even today, in many industries the richness of the information flow allows the customer to choose product features (color, functionality, and so on) before the product is actually made, without the manufacturer incurring extra costs or time delays. General Motors envisions a time when customers will be able to choose car features using Web-based technology that directly communicates their choices to the factory. It is not beyond reason to believe that future customers will be able to "design" major parts of the look and feel of their cars in real time as the car is moving through the building process.

Match Preferences

Two alternatives for matching preferences have emerged: personal and social profiling. A *personal profile* builds an understanding of each individual directly. What areas are of interest to that customer and what knowledge does that customer need and when? Usually, it is the end user who identifies the key requirements for assembling a knowledge package. For example, the workers on oil drilling platforms want information about how to unstick pipes. They have little use for knowledge about supply chain problems in refineries or the latest lessons learned in the construction of gas stations. They have even less need for information on the fast food retail stores attached to them. Furthermore, they want to see the information in videos rather than on the printed page. Their needs may reflect their job requirements, their training, and their level of experience. A personal profile allows such distinctions in the packaging process.

In a Web-based environment, anyone can submit key word searches and characteristics or issues to filter and find those knowledge assets that will be particularly useful. Technology solutions referred to as *intelligent agents*, such as PointCast and others, are tools that can help individuals and groups target knowledge assets.

An intelligent agent is a software program designed to search for content that matches the parameters that the user provides (Maes, Guttman, and Moukas, 1999). Once armed with these preferences, the agent constantly scans knowledge repositories. When a *hit* is scored, the item found matches the parameters specified and it is retrieved and becomes part of the user's knowledge base. Evolving technology allows users to have a dialogue with this agent, communicating the usefulness of each item retrieved and thereby increasing the probability that the next items retrieved will be an even better match. Over time, search agents learn about the preferences of the people that use them.

We realize that the intelligent agent blurs the line between the push strategy and the pull strategy. The analogy for a pull strategy would be sending out a search party looking for information with specific parameters. If an individual communicates constantly with the search party—accepting, qualifying, or rejecting what is found—the search party gets better and better at finding what the person wants. The end user is pulling that information.

In contrast, the search party may have no contact with the end user after being given an initial assignment. The information found will be *pushed* back to the person requesting it. In either case, the unique needs and desires of the person making the request determine how the knowledge should be consolidated, packaged, and delivered.

Principle 5.1

Strive to capture individual customer data and use it to target knowledge.

In recent years a new technique has emerged for targeting preferences; it is known as *social profiling*. Social profiling determines what is of most interest and use to an individual, not by profiling that person but by profiling the community to which that person belongs (Goldberg, Nichols, Oki, and Terry, 1992). Preferences are discovered as members of the community interact with one another as much as through their collective characteristics. These communities are formed around common interests. When one individual discovers something, every member in the community with a similar profile is alerted to the available information. Amazon.com is a good example of a company that uses social profiling. When users search for a book at Amazon.com, they can read reviews written by other readers. Once they order a book, they are automatically put into a community of people who have bought that same type of book. Book purchasers are thus categorized according to demographic characteristics based on the type of book. If a customer with similar characteristics reviews another book favorably Amazon.com immediately alerts those in the community that the review and the book are available. Amazon.com may also invite certain purchasers to write more book reviews based on the usefulness of their recommendations in the community. Certain people might write very insightful reviews that increase the probability of sales to others.

In sum, it is as if a friend who likes the same kinds of things as you do is recommending a good book. Of course, people have long bought books at the suggestion of friends; word-of-mouth advertising is a powerful marketing force. With the advent of the Internet, "word of mouse" only enhances this phenomenon. The concept of social profiling simply harnesses this force in a systematic manner.

The more people who read and review a book, the more refined Amazon.com's knowledge base becomes. The more a reader buys, the more it knows about him or her and the closer it can get when making recommendations. Furthermore, by collecting data on purchasers of reviewed books, Amazon.com knows not only what group to put people in, but how likely they are to be swayed by the opinions of others in the group. It can increase its campaign efforts to get the information to certain individuals.

> ## Principle 5.2
>
> *If you can place a customer in a definable interest group, use social profiling to target knowledge.*

Choosing between personal profiling or social profiling is the first targeting choice. Do you package and deliver knowledge based on what the individual or the group is like? Do personal preferences or community preferences prevail?

Find the Right Packaging

The main objective of the targeting phase is to develop a customer-driven approach for knowledge sharing. After determining the consumers' preferences, the company must determine how to deliver the information. There are two basic approaches to packaging: sequential and linked. A *sequential* strategy assumes that the consumer will take a more passive role. The sequential packaging approach lays knowledge out in a predetermined format and sequence. For example, chapters are put into a book in sequence. In contrast, a *linked* strategy gives consumers the ability to weave together what they want and in effect determine their own packaging. The ultimate sequence is therefore not predefined.

Sequential strategies are the more common. Most of the documents, reports, and papers we receive are delivered in a predetermined format, a sequential strategy. The Center for Army Lessons Learned offers a good example of this kind of packaging. CALL responded to a sudden increase in mine-related injuries in Bosnia by producing a concise briefing booklet that conveyed the lessons learned, what to do, and what not to do. CALL consolidated the lessons learned and best practices embedded in its database, printed the booklet, and then distributed it to all soldiers in a matter of days from when the need became apparent. Merck's Heart Care Network also presented information in a predetermined format and then delivered it to hospitals and doctors for their use. Other examples of this packaging strategy are company newsletters, reports from analysts, briefing papers, and so on. Such strategies need not be limited to paper. BP regularly produces videos of lessons learned that feature local experts relaying their experiences; as we noted earlier, the workers on its oil drilling platforms prefer the videos to printed material. Thus, properly presented, knowledge that is prepackaged and delivered to the point of decision making can be very valuable. However, end users who use it are put into a passive consumer role. They can either accept or reject what is presented, but they cannot alter it.

Principle 5.3

Package knowledge in a sequential format if you are clear about what knowledge people need and when and how they need it.

With the advent of hypertext, or networked technologies, a new and powerful packaging alternative exists. A hypertext document allows key concepts and phrases to be networked to other content. The content designer creates direct links from knowledge in one area to knowledge in another. The consumer can then simply click on a highlighted word or phrase and automatically travel to a new, related content area. Made popular by browser technologies on the Internet such as Netscape, this technology has emerged as a powerful tool for allowing consumers to bundle relevant knowledge content in the way they want to see it and use it. In essence, the designer can create a node of content in a knowledge web in which the hot links create the paths that connect each node in the network. The consumer then chooses the path to follow.

Early uses of this linked targeting strategy were quite simple. A document might include links to reference materials or footnotes. As readers scanned the document, they could go to a source document or footnote to gather more detailed data. In that document they might find another footnote that captured their interest and go off again on another search. On the World Wide Web, the linked strategy allows the user to navigate quickly through various parts of Web sites based on personal preferences. The Web does not provide fixed documents but rather a network of knowledge assets in which readers maintain control over what they see and use. A linked strategy offers much more than mobility between documents or elements within a document. It allows the customer to become an active designer of the packaging content.

Xerox's Eureka Project, already discussed in Chapter 4, is a good example. It constructed a system that allows service technicians to download tips from others on how to fix a certain machine part. When they search for these tips, they find hot links to other information sources that can provide more in-depth information on that part, the whole system, long-term versus short-term fixes, explanations of new services and technology available, and so on. The consumers—in this case, the technicians—determine what knowledge is woven together and how to produce the knowledge bundle that they finally use.

Principle 5.4

Package knowledge in a linked format if users need to search and create their own configurations.

Choices: Targeting Knowledge to Get It Where, When, and How It Is Needed

When you combine the customization and configuration strategies described here, you can identify your choices for targeting knowledge appropriately. Figure 5.1 illustrates how the various strategies can be combined.

Figure 5.1

Choosing the Knowledge-Targeting Strategy

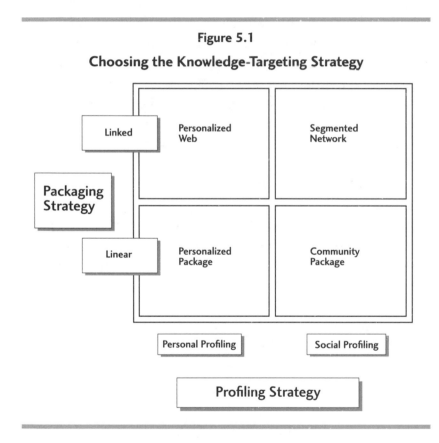

Linear Packaging/Personal Profiling: Personalized Package

With a linear packaging strategy, the documents and information are made available in a predetermined sequence and format. The customer does not have the ability to search and create a different knowledge product. But before they are delivered, the products can be customized to fit personal preferences. Here, the objective is to get the best knowledge products to each individual consumer, to provide each with a customized package. Through personal profiling, a firm can predict what information a consumer will find most useful. For example, based on your age, family situation, income level, and expenditure patterns Fidelity can guess which financial services might interest you most. It can then send you material that meets your needs through the mail or electronically. Amazon.com does the same on its Web site. You provide a profile of characteristics and interests and the company provides you with the documents that match those interests. By *personalized packaging* we mean customizing knowledge assets to *match personal preferences* and delivering those assets using traditional text or multimedia documents.

Linear Packaging/Social Profiling: Community Package

The term social profiling highlights the concept that the relevance of a knowledge asset is determined through some community-based process. The package within which it is presented is determined by the community's needs. By *community packaging* we mean using an *understanding of social groups* and communities to define relevant content and deliver it through traditional text or multimedia documents. As we saw earlier in this chapter, Amazon.com uses this strategy. It uses individual preferences and personal book evaluations to locate a community of people with similar interests and tastes. All the company needs to do is watch what books people buy based on the recommendations it sends them, and it can put them into evermore specific communities. Within these increasingly narrow categories, people will receive more recommendations and so on. Thus, people get recommendations on books that fit their interests while Amazon.com gets an ongoing learning tool to continually refine its profile of its readers, and hence what it will recommend to them in the future.

Linked Packaging/Personal Profiling: Personalized Web

Combining a linked packaging approach with personal profiling allows a firm to filter the content available for the consumer and create a personalized web. By *personalized web* we mean packaging customized content in a way that allows an individual to *flexibly navigate* and explore. In the extreme, this combination of strategies can create a unique web for each individual. For example, a feature on Fidelity's Web site—**www.fidelity.com**—allows its most active investors access to their own customized knowledge assets. The system provides a knowledge web for each investor. Based on personal information and preferences, an investor can access her account information, related industry analysis, customized tracking, and trend analysis of stocks, and designate the types of news reports that will be pushed her way. She sets the parameters, and the Web gives her access to a wide range of assets networked together. She can search and create her own knowledge package quickly and she can do it every day.

If a customer clicks on a particular stock, a link to an analyst's report on the stock is instantaneously available. The customer must choose to travel that link, but once she does, she will find links to other economic data that can provide an even fuller picture. With continued use, the system will begin to reconfigure itself as it learns what the customer wants. A web of knowledge grows that is not only customized for what the consumer wants today but is able to anticipate what she might want tomorrow.

Linked Packaging/Social Profiling: Segmented Network

More and more organizations are discovering the power of using linked packaging with social profiling. They can provide users with a web of knowledge based on the communities to which they belong. By *segmented network* we mean using community characteristics to create a *web of content* that can be flexibly navigated and explored.

ICEX is an Internet company that develops such knowledge products for corporations. Its customers identify a topic of interest and ICEX creates a webbed set of knowledge products that allow them control over what they read at any given time. A key element of ICEX's method is first identifying the social reference group that defines the relevant content. They then use experts within the reference group to define key knowledge areas and construct a knowledge web the customer can explore. ICEX also provides a range of links that allow customers to go deeper into any given topic, explore new related material, access reference documents, and gather knowledge from lessons learned by others. The company is constantly updating by adding links to new material, customer surveys, research reports, and information on best practices.

ICEX makes sure that what it adds is relevant by having those in the community it is serving evaluate potential new material. These experts not only filter out low-quality content but also help ensure that it is appropriately linked to the existing material. Thus, the customer receives a knowledge web that has been judged to be relevant by a broader community. The networked community strategy allows the customer to maintain control over what he sees but at the same time to have a rich set of knowledge products available that are likely to prove useful. Thus, this is an interesting combination of push and pull strategies, and one that is likely to become even more prevalent as the technology develops further.

Principle 5.5

Choose the targeting strategy, preferences, and packaging that best customize the knowledge assets to meet the consumer's needs.

Moving Forward

The question for the leader is which strategy to choose. Once again the answer is to choose the one that will give you the greatest impact. No approach is better than the others. Each has advantages and disadvantages and must be managed carefully to provide optimum payoff. Choose wisely, but choose. The worst option is to assume that what you are doing is meeting the customer's needs. Amazon.com would waste considerable money if it merely sent a bunch of documents to users. The only hope for Amazon.com and other such companies to be profitable is to focus on the community and use the community to drive what it does. Fidelity would not be able to meet its customers' needs if it only provided packaged reports. Push the knowledge that consumers need to them and you will improve their satisfaction and performance.

Reflect

The View from Above

AS THE WORLD becomes more integrated, more complex, and faster, the leadership challenge is to understand more clearly how things fit together. Kenneth Boulding (1953) proposed viewing organizations as systems:

⇨ With results from one event feeding back and becoming the input and guide for the next event
⇨ With results from one entity becoming input for other entities
⇨ With lower-order systems creating the foundation for higher-order systems

Similarly, Chris Argyris (1977) talked about double-loop learning. The first loop relates to understanding what is affecting perform-ance. The second loop relates to understanding the assumptions that are made and the mental models that are used to interpret sur-rounding events. Argyris argued that most of the recommendations of current management theories do not adequately account for both loops. In particular, they do not encourage awareness of the higher-level systems that determine what we pay attention to.

The same issue comes up in the tension between seeking effi-ciency (doing things right), and seeking effectiveness (doing the right things). If we remain at the lower level of learning we continue to learn how to improve on what we are doing. We may get better and better at it, but we run the risk of getting better and better at the wrong thing. Thus, leaders need to ask not only how to improve what they are doing but also what they should be doing (Schon, 1984).

The need for learning loops—using what happens in one period of time to guide our thinking and action in the next—has been part of good management for a long time. When we formulate a strategy it is always necessary to go to a higher level and question how we see the world and what we are doing. Planning, budgeting, and financial systems are based on the assumption that the better we understand what has happened, the better we can predict what will happen.

In the fast cycle of the new economy we still need to understand the past. The past provides the foundation on which we move forward; we need to capture learning from our experience and use it to plan our future. What has changed is the complexity of the world we need to understand and the speed with which we must understand it. The advantage accrues to those who have the ability to learn and adapt, to understand the whole, and to evolve effectively. Our cycle of learning—moving from knowledge-to-performance and back—has to be faster than the speed of change. This capability is key to a sustainable advantage.

Yet, in a world of complexity, speed, and changing relationships we must take time to reflect. By *reflect* we mean to gain a higher-order view. To reflect we need to get the proper perspective on the field of action and understand the nature and extent of change.

The View from the Balcony

Often you can reflect best when you rise above the action and see all the pieces and how they fit together. We briefly mentioned Ron Heifetz's (1994, p. 253) balcony analogy in Chapter 1. Heifetz suggests that you imagine that you are on a dance floor dancing a waltz with a wonderful partner. Next, imagine what the scene would look like if you were on the balcony above, watching all the dancing pairs as they swirl across the floor. Your focus would shift to the whole rather than to the pieces. If the dancers are really good, they will adjust when the music unexpectedly changes to a rumba, and you will see a whole different pattern. Now, the challenge for leaders: imagine being on the dance floor engaged in the dance but still responsible for understanding and leading the dance as a whole. The vantage point from which you do your part makes it just about impossible to see and understand the whole. As Heifetz says, "Our attention is captured by the music, our partner, and the need to sense the dancing space of others nearby to stay off their toes." To discern the larger patterns on the dance floor—who is dancing with whom, in what groups, in what location, and who is sitting out which dance—we have to stop moving ourselves and get up on the balcony.

The same is true in organizations. Every once in a while you need to gain a higher-level view that allows you to validate and integrate what you are seeing. You get an expanded view of your supply chain by getting above the action. You expand your view to see how the pieces inside and outside the organization fit together.

Curtis Davis is the head of product development in the transportation division of Analog Devices (Baird, Holland, and Deacon, 1999), a division that develops signal components used by logistics organizations to run shipping stations. Engineers and computer experts are assigned to twenty-seven different teams, each responsible for a different product and customer. Even though these teams are working on different applications of the company's technology, many of the problems they face and solutions they find are common. They all use the same product development process. Davis was looking for a way to improve not only the quality of the products but also the speed with which they were developed. He decided that if he could just get the teams to stop and think about what they were doing and how they were doing it, performance would improve. He included as part of the product development process a requirement that on a weekly basis the teams stop, get on the balcony, identify what they had learned, and apply the learning back into the next steps of the product development process. The simple act of stopping and acquiring learning drove product improvement and time spent by 10 percent. But the big improvement came when the teams started integrating what they learned. By going to a higher level and looking across teams, Davis and his leadership team were able not only to get one team applying what others had learned but also to validate what was being done and consolidate what was learned across teams. By identifying trends and solutions across teams they were able to improve the product and look critically at the product development process itself. Knowledge began to build on itself. The product development teams at the company now integrate and consolidate what they have learned at three different levels, thus getting up on even higher balconies. On the first balcony they look at what a product development team has been doing for a certain time period. On the second balcony they look at what has been happening across product development teams. Finally, on the third balcony they look at the whole product development process over time across the whole organization.

> ### Principle 6.1
>
> *Create and assume a leadership role that includes the responsibility to view and integrate action and learning across multiple units.*

Aggregating Learning

The U.S. Army has a unique way of getting everyone to take a higher-level view. They refer to it as the *murder board* (remember, this is the military). The murder board is nothing more than a compilation of sticky notes posted on a big board. Each note contains a brief description of a lesson learned. After the notes have been posted, the organizers consolidate them into larger categories. The ones that do not fit or add little value are "murdered."

The Tritec team at Chrysler modified this approach to look critically at their own product development process. The team identified twenty-one key learnings from their experience. The next question was how to consolidate what they had learned. For example, a number of learnings related to getting people to communicate at the beginning of the project. They aggregated these learnings and referred to the category as the *payoffs of co-location*. Trying to achieve perspective from an even higher level, Chrysler then asked what it was about co-location that drove performance. The answer was that it made it easier to resolve conflicts and other issues sooner. The Tritec team labeled the learning this way: aggressively facilitate communication early in the project. It took only two hours for the team to consolidate the twenty-one learnings into five categories.

In an endeavor like Chrysler's, it is important that the right people are involved. That means including people with different perspectives who have viewed the situations over time. The Tritec team included people from throughout the product development process as well as people from design and engineering in their early meetings. Everyone had an equal voice, and everyone was responsible for producing the higher-level learnings. Tool 7 shows the actual announcement of the program, which explains the setup and the procedures the Tritec team used.

Tool 7
LEARNING AGGREGATION

OVERVIEW

We have two purposes in this session: (1) to capture and name the high-level learnings, and (2) to push the management team to describe the value of these learnings.

PREPARATION

We will have prepared on 3" x 5" cards the name of each of the 21 original learnings, plus the names of new learnings, added via the management interviews. These will be laid out, ungrouped, on a 3' x 6' foot table.

Time	Agenda
3:00–3:10	**Overview** Explain the process, ground rules of the session, desired output.
3:10–3:25	**Group Grouping Session** All individual learning cards will be grouped by the team gathering around the table. Speed versus deliberation is the order of the day. Anyone can move any card; consensus will emerge. Not all cards need to find homes. There should be no more than 5 to 6 groupings.
3:25–3:50	**Creating Header Cards** Teams are to look for the card in each grouping that captures the central idea and move it to top, or create a concise 3- to 5-word header that summarizes the grouping.

3:50–4:30	**Value Session** As the final test of the value of their summaries, push them to justify the summaries. "What has this done for you? How has it helped the bottom line of cost, quality, and timeliness? Explain why." Push for examples. Capture on flip chart.
4:30–4:40	**Individual Rankings** With groupings on the board, give everyone 3 red dots and tell them to put them next to the most important learnings. This is one more filter that forces a value decision and should reduce the total to fewer than 5 key learnings.
4:40–5:00	**Take Action** "OK, if this is so good, what can we start doing right now to make it work for us in the project now?"
5:00–5:15	**Summary** Here are the 3 to 5 key higher-level learnings for phase one. These are things that we have done that really had an impact. Here is how they have had an impact. Here is why. And here is what we can do about them right now, to get even better.

This exercise gets everyone involved in consolidating data to form knowledge together. It also allows everyone to provide their own perspective. One person's insight is no more or less important than another's. The key is what emerges from the combination of all of their contributions. The exercise is designed to help a group work together in identifying higher-level learnings. The same process can be used by an individual, but at the risk of missing some important learning because of the single perspective.

Being Both In and Out of the Action

The leadership challenge is to be both active and reflective, to manage the ebb and flow between action and knowledge, to be both in and out of the action. Acquiring, structuring, and targeting knowledge are activities that most often take place "in the game." They are hard to do, but at least they are part of the action process. In contrast, focusing and reflecting are "out of the game" and they are even harder to do. Focusing comes somewhat naturally because we have long been indoctrinated to establish a goal, put a strategy in place, and manage a plan. However, reflecting—taking time to get a higher-level perspective on what has been done and what can be learned—is, unfortunately, often seen as wasting time. We live in such an action-oriented culture that taking any time at all away from doing seems like a dereliction of duty. The pressures of time in the new economy are so great that our natural tendency when a task is completed is to move quickly to the next. Worse yet, when we are in the action we believe that stopping to think is impossible.

In a fast-cycle world, many do not have the time to take time out. But they do have time to step back and reflect. Lieutenant Colonel Hal Moore is someone who learned how to get up on the balcony, literally in the heat of battle (Sullivan and Harper, 1997). Back in 1965, he led the 1st Battalion, 7th Cavalry, into the Ia Drang Valley of the central highlands of Vietnam. In the first major clash between U.S. forces and the North Vietnamese, Moore led his troops into a long-time communist stronghold, where they were quickly surrounded and outnumbered by four or five to one. In the end, "Moore's command had distinguished itself against an enemy that was far superior in numbers and that had held the initiative throughout much of the battle. Ultimately, both sides would claim victory, but the tenacity of the 7th Cavalry and its indomitable spirit are a monument to effective leadership" (Sullivan and Harper, 1997, p. 46).

However, there was a mystery in the commander's behavior: "During the fight, Moore established his command post in the center of the primary landing zone, partially protected by a large termite hill.

With his radio operators, forward observers, and others he worked the artillery, air support, and resupply while he led the battalion in fight. From time to time he was observed to withdraw, appearing to those around him to be shutting down and blocking them out for brief periods of time" (Sullivan and Harper, 1997, p. 46).

What was Moore doing during those moments of withdrawal? After the battle, Moore and his men were debriefed in detail to draw lessons about how the North Vietnamese had fought. When asked about his periods of seeming withdrawal, Moore said that he had been reflecting, asking himself three questions (p. 47):

⇨ What is happening?
⇨ What is not happening?
⇨ What can I do to influence the action?

Moore's behavior is the essence of reflection. He was scanning his environment, integrating what was happening in the whole field of action, and then determining his best course. The purpose was to win the battle, not simply parry each thrust. The genius in Moore's approach lies in his second question. By getting on the balcony and reflecting on what was not happening, he was able to open his mind to broader opportunities, to see the full range of his options. He was better able to anticipate what might or might not happen next and to plan his moves to the best advantage: a critical lesson that helped not only in this battle but in many future events in his life.

Principle 6.2

Get out of the action so you can capture a higher-level view and then get back into the action quickly.

Seeking Patterns, Repetitions, and Relationships

Our work suggests that leaders can establish several different reflective processes. Each helps frame different issues. Each focuses attention in different ways and leads to different insights. In this sense, each method is biased, systematically skewing outcomes in predictable ways. But bias is not necessarily bad. All high-performing systems are perspective-biased. Bias becomes bad when we do not recognize the existence and nature of the bias. Then, the systematic skewing of a point of view will dig a rut for the individual, the team, and ultimately, the organization. If the rut gets too deep it will obscure all else and ultimately lead to failure. The challenge is to balance different approaches to the reflective process, using each to achieve its unique benefit, while gaining from the combination. Our view of the whole is influenced by our *perspective* and the *degree of change*.

Inside or Outside Perspective

First, perspective defines where the boundaries of the systems we are considering will be drawn and whether we are looking at the inside or outside of the unit (Churchman, 1983). Each reflective process must define what is in and what is out. Much like a photographer who chooses what he will focus on and what he will leave in the background, the leader must choose a focus.

Normally, the "inside" refers to the day-to-day space of action faced by the performing unit. Attention is directed toward those engaged in the activity. Most often the one source of information to support this perspective is that of those involved in the situation. But the experience of the immediate actors establishes bias, because the world is seen through their eyes. This is both a strength and a weakness. It will most likely surface solutions and actions that the key individuals will understand and implement. This very pragmatic and concrete result of the internal reflective process makes it quite appealing and reasonably easy to implement. In fact, its biggest danger is that it is so easy to do it will drive out all other methods of reflection.

At the other end of the continuum, approaches to reflection take an outside perspective. What is happening in the environment and how does that affect what we are doing in here? The externally oriented methods begin by focusing attention on actions and actors that are not directly involved in internal activities. Mason and Mitroff (1981) developed a process they term *stakeholder analysis*. It is a reflective process that begins by focusing attention on a key stakeholder outside the organization and how that person influences action inside the organization. The intent is to understand better how outside forces affect the way work should be designed or resources allocated.

The biggest virtue of this approach is that it forces you to see the world from a broader perspective. You must confront the complexity and perhaps threatening reality of the environment in which you work. The limitation of this approach is that it can often be overwhelming, creating a big gap between the insights generated and pragmatic action that can be taken. The action-oriented leader may resist trying to understand the larger context, claiming lack of time and the likelihood that whatever is discovered will be too removed from the action. Of course, if a leader does not understand what is "out there" he runs the risk of taking action that seems good from his limited perspective but has little meaning in the grand scheme.

Incremental or Quantum Change

Second, perspective is influenced by the degree of change you are trying to understand. Are you trying to improve what you are doing, or are you questioning whether you should even be doing it? Are you looking for incremental change or quantum change? It is quite common today to hear about "thinking outside the box." Thomas Kuhn (1996), in his seminal work on the nature of scientific revolutions, argued that change comes incrementally until we get to the point where the platform from which we work and interpret the world collapses. Then we have to shift our mental model and behaviors totally in what is often referred to as a paradigm shift. The extent to which we look for or are open to a paradigm shift influences how we reflect on what has happened and how we implement what we discover. Larry Greiner (1998) argued along similar lines in his article about organizational evolution versus revolution. He proposed that organizations evolve incrementally but periodically experience revolutionary change. The challenge for the leader is to understand when evolution versus revolution is occurring (or required) and how to drive the appropriate transformation process. Each requires a different perspective. In Greiner's words, "We may even see companies with dual organizational structures: a habit structure for getting the daily work done and a reflective structure for stimulating new perspectives" (p. 64).

The Internet and related technologies have created an environment in which many organizations need to make major changes. Christensen (1997) called this the *innovator's dilemma* created by the emergence of a disruptive technology. He argued that the leader makes the tough choice of shifting to a new business platform while dismantling any systems that have led to the organization's success. How does the leader come to understand the organization is, in fact, in such a dilemma rather than simply experiencing a passing fad? How do leaders engage in a reflective process that enables them to understand and make the change in a timely fashion?

Our second dimension, degree of change, goes from *pattern recognition*, where we are looking for small incremental improvement, to *transformation*, where we try to find quantum changes.

In pattern recognition, the challenge is to connect the dots, perhaps even rearrange the links between the dots. The observer looks across contexts, attempting to surface the trends or broader issues that give rise to the observed behavior or phenomenon. The tools of pattern recognition are quite familiar today. We use sophisticated, analytical tools to spot trends, associations, and clusters. Data mining, for example, provides powerful algorithms for matching and correlating events. These tools propose patterns, enabling the user to see a broader process. An empirical orientation is common to these approaches. Whether based on subjective assessments by experts or quantitative analysis of a megadatabase, most pattern recognition processes use experience or past behavior (in the form of data, stories, personal histories, and so on) as the foundation for discovery.

But what if a company faces a discontinuity? In today's world, even the most efficient process for trying to pick out patterns will flounder. Why look for patterns of current behavior when what you should look for are radical changes that are beginning to happen? In this case, you are using the reflective process to look for transformation.

A worldview is a highly interrelated set of beliefs and assumptions. This core set of assumptions allows the individual and, hence, the organization to make sense of the dynamic, chaotic world. But as Kuhn (1996) argues, as the world and our knowledge of it evolves, new systems of belief emerge that prove to be more effective—that is, lead to a stronger, more predictable link between behavior and outcomes. When large changes happen, the leader must help the members of the organization challenge their own beliefs and their current success in order to create an environment in which revolutionary change can occur. In recent years, we have seen design concepts—such as the total quality movement, reengineering, and knowledge management—provide processes to help organizations transform themselves. In all these efforts, the leader's role is as much to shift how people think as what they do. If people simply carry out their new activities with their old mindset, change will not last.

Choices: Knowing What to Look For

We do not argue that all situations require transformational change. Such approaches are resource-intensive and very disruptive. The leader must choose when to look for patterns and when to react to transformational change. Once again, choices must be made. We have defined four different approaches to the reflective process:

searching for *performance patterns, the competitive landscape, weak signals,* or *thin threads.* Each approach has its own unique benefits. Figure 6.1 illustrates how the various approaches can be combined.

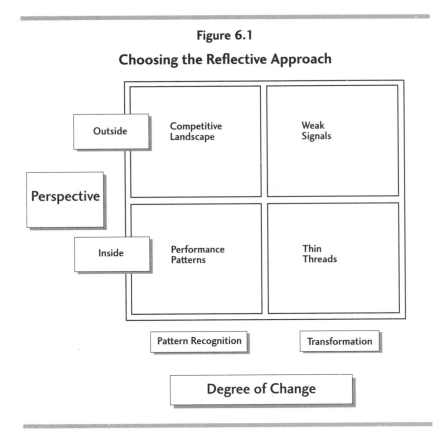

Figure 6.1

Choosing the Reflective Approach

Pattern Recognition/Inside Focus:
Performance Patterns

We begin with internal pattern recognition: learning from watching what is happening on the job. By *performance patterns* we mean the capability to recognize *incremental changes* that drive performance improvement. Not surprisingly, executives, team leaders, and individuals feel quite comfortable with this approach. Much as has been done in total quality management and organizational learning, this approach requires the leader to create a climate in which thinking and reflection are part of everyone's job. Total quality management provides us with numerous examples and methodologies for individuals and teams to reflect systematically on their experiences in an effort to improve performance. There is a wealth of evidence to support the claim that these processes lead to significant local improvements. More difficult, however, is to see the extent to which these individual experiences can be integrated to discover broader, more systematic trends. The more it can be systematized the better your chance of capturing higher-level learnings. The process at Analog Computers, described earlier, is iterative, each time trying to achieve a broader and higher level view on which to capture the patterns in the company's internal processes. But the focus is still the same, identifying within the work itself and across the stages of product development the opportunities that drive incremental development.

Transformation/Inside Focus:
Thin Threads

Even in a world of transformational change, things sometimes take time. The typical method of portraying a transformational change is as a discontinuous change, a single giant step forward. But organizations do not work that way. They change one or two components at a time; the trick is perceiving which component will drive the big changes. *Thin threads* are changes in a *single process* within the organization or a group of activities that identify the discontinuity that is coming, and establish changes that "create a foothold for the future" (Sullivan and Harper, 1997, p. 177). The challenge is to pick components that are significant enough that they will pull others along.

In Boston, billions of dollars are being spent to submerge the expressway that runs through the city. In its place will appear parks and walkways. The key to the whole project is a massive suspension bridge that leads the traffic over the rivers and into the submerged highway. Rising out of the ground is a giant wishbone through which massive cables will be strung to support one of the world's largest suspension bridges. When the support structure is ready, a small cable will be threaded through it to pull a larger cable, which will in turn pull a still-larger cable. The process will continue with each cable pulling a larger one until the massive suspension cables, which by themselves are impossible to manipulate, will be pulled through and attached. The thin threads make the massive transformation possible.

When you try to understand the paradigm shifts, your thought processes work the same way. You search for the thin threads that lead the way. A good example of a thin tread is the fast-cycle prototyping organizations do to investigate new procedures or products. The philosophy is simple: try something out that offers a quick win and provides quick learning. After that, you can commit larger resources. Look for the trends that will have an impact on what you can do in the future.

Pattern Recognition/Outside Focus: Competitive Landscape

Here the leader looks outside the organization to find implications for action. What is happening in the environment and how does it affect what we should be doing? By *competitive landscape* we mean the capability to *systematically explore competitors'* and other stakeholders' activities in order to anticipate market conditions. Benchmarking is a tool often used by firms to scan externally. Consulting firms also provide strategic analysis of competitive markets to support this reflective process. General Motors, for example, spends considerable energy and resources on benchmarking and analysis scanning the global markets both to understand the actions of its competitors and to identify and interpret emerging events that would affect its businesses. No matter what approach is taken, the key is to remember that the purpose is to add an external perspective to the lessons learned emerging from within the firm. For example, the growth of MP3 and Napster give a record company a different framework for interpreting and understanding what is happening within the firm from a radically difference perspective.

Transformation/Outside Focus:
Weak Signals

But what about emerging events that are outside the traditional view of the automotive industry? How can General Motors create the mechanisms for its leaders to challenge their assumptions, to shift out of their current mental model? This challenge leads us to a significantly different reflective context in which reflection means envisioning a future that may be inconsistent with past experiences. Current information systems and measures may be the very reason why we are unable to "see" an emerging phenomenon. And yet, bringing to bear the knowledge assets of the firm to support this type of reflection may be crucial to the survival of the firm, particularly during highly volatile times. You have to look for the *weak signals* that portend things to come. By *weak signals* we mean emerging knowledge or lessons learned that are *early indicators of transformation* changes coming.

In searching for weak signals, processes are needed to help the leader challenge the traditional wisdom and its underlying beliefs and assumptions. What emerging trends may have a significant impact and the power to change the competitive rules of the game? Mason and Mitroff (1981) recognized this key requirement in the ongoing process of strategic thinking through their method of assumption surfacing. In this process, the leader focuses on shareholders of policy or strategy—that is, those who can influence or will be affected by the firm's strategy—and for each group surfaces the critical assumptions held about those shareholders. For example, a drug manufacturer may believe that prescribing doctors will focus on the effectiveness of a drug rather than its cost. The methodology systematically challenges critical assumptions in order to explore future business scenarios that might emerge. Data are then gathered to support or refute the emergence of such a business context. Thus, the assumption, "The doctor will focus more on price than on effectiveness," leads to a vastly different view of market strategies and pricing strategies than the more traditional assumption, "The doctor will focus on patient care." This reflective process often does not end with a final design. It merely encourages efforts to focus on weak signals. Once weak signals are identified, the firm can then run strategic experiments to test the validity and robustness of the signals that have been located. Perhaps the leader should invest in the product of a small company that is immersed in this market opportunity. Why? To learn—to create a flow of knowledge that can help inform the strategic learning agenda.

General Motors Company's development of Onstar (Venkatraman and Henderson, 1998) provides a good example. We already mentioned Onstar in Chapter 1; it is the cellular phone–based system that links drivers to a service center. Cars are equipped with a global positioning device so the service center knows their exact location. Thus, emergency aid can be dispatched, directions conveyed, and service requests routed to the closest dealer. In the very earliest stages of this product's development, this capability was viewed primarily as a feature that would differentiate high-end models. It would be offered to customers with a desire for the service, much like those who like to install very high-end sound systems. But transformational perspective views the Onstar system not as a feature of a car but rather as a way to link the car to the World Wide Web. Looking at it this way, GM now has the opportunity to allow millions of Internet users to connect to the Web when they have time on their hands.

How would you think about this opportunity? What is its potential? Who are your real competitors? What do you know and what do you need to know to develop and execute strategy in this context? GM aggressively pursued a different reflective processes. The company built a simulation model that both aggregated data in relevant ways and helped the leadership explore new assumptions and business models. They used this model in combination with a strategic decision-making process that allowed them to understand this opportunity in the face of very weak and uncertain market signals. As time evolved, they used this process to seek out expertise that could help define strategic alternatives. Through this process they identified alternatives quite different from those emerging from traditional analyses of the auto industry. Of course, as they began to fully recognize the potential of Onstar and the role of the World Wide Web for the company and the industry, the GM leadership had to take action. These actions required radically different processes and work flows. They found themselves needing to lead transformational change.

Moving Forward

Performance patterns, the competitive landscape, weak signals, and thin threads are all valuable indicators that provide useful examples of how knowledge capability can drive a company's strategic focus. However, each one leads to different results. The mistake many organizations make in their knowledge initiatives is to miss the linkage and find no clear reason for their actions. Leaders should choose the focus and then the methods and processes to use to evaluate progress and continually test the focus. That is the essence of strategic learning. Failure to choose the method that best frames the reflective process will ultimately undermine any knowledge initiative. After all, if the knowledge engine only works at the bottom of the organization, people who aspire to reach the top will soon spend their time on something else.

A common feature of all the successful knowledge initiatives we studied was the belief that the lessons learned at the point of action might influence the leadership of the firm. The knowledge engine must drive the whole organization. Leaders must take the time for reflection or very few will deem it important. It simply is too hard to pull away from the action and believe a view from above matters if the leader does not use what is discovered.

Principle 6.3

Match the reflective process (inside or out-side perspective, incremental or quantum change) to meet the performance demands of the situation.

People must also understand which perspective they are using to view the situation and the biases it creates. Individuals and organizations usually focus on understanding performance patterns. Total quality management has drilled into us the importance of capturing quality problems and fixing them. In many organizations it has become a natural part of doing business. But if we focus only on performance patterns, that will cause us to miss the larger shifts happening in our relationships with others and the bigger system in which we fit. We will also miss the weak signals that indicate the shifts are already happening and the thin threads that allow us to make needed changes.

In most situations, all these perspectives are needed. Once you are up on the balcony looking in all directions, the challenge is to combine the views to develop a perspective that not only helps you understand what is being learned and how the focus should be adjusted in the present but also what is coming in the future and how best to adapt and adjust.

Of all the leader's responsibilities in the new economy, reflecting is the hardest, but it also provides the greatest payoff. Furthermore, you cannot go up on the balcony only once a year. You have to be both in and out of the game continually. The speed with which you can climb up there, capture what you see, adjust your focus, and move back to action will determine your success. Knowledge initiatives will not be sustained over time unless the leader personally creates and leverages knowledge assets.

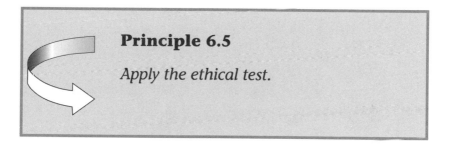

Principle 6.4

To sustain knowledge initiatives over time, leaders must actively use the knowledge assets that have been created.

Reflection also provides an opportunity to challenge assumptions, beliefs, and values. When you take the ethical test, you ask yourself a simple question: Based on what I now see, what others have told me, and on the higher-level learnings I have gained, am I still comfortable with my assumptions, beliefs, and values, or should they change? Only from the balcony can you gain the perspective you need to answer this question.

Principle 6.5

Apply the ethical test.

Moving to Action

LET US END where we began. The knowledge engine is not about e-commerce, dot.coms, knowledge management, or technology. All these are important phenomena but they are also only indications of much bigger things. Soon the "e" will be dropped from electronic commerce and it will just be the way business is done. The "dot" will disappear from dot commerce because the Internet will be so prevalent no one will even think about it. What we refer to as knowledge management will go the way of total quality management: not the responsibility of specialized departments or big consulting firms, but simply the way work gets done. We are entering a knowledge economy where every interaction with a customer will have to produce a new understanding of that customer. Every opportunity to perform will also have to provide an opportunity to learn. Everything we learn will have to be quickly applied back into the organization. What one unit knows will have to be quickly available to every other unit. And what you do today will have to be the foundation of what you do in the future. Already, we do not have the time. The competitive pressures are too high and the resources too scarce to make the same mistake over again. Remember the motto at Xerox, "Never make the same mistake once."

Creating and leveraging knowledge assets is not an option, it is a necessity. Yes, the economy has room for well-run and efficient factories that produce goods and services. Moving money from one organization to another to drive growth and innovation is important. But the value will be created and captured by those who have a strategic orientation and know how to produce the knowledge that will help drive that orientation. And it is the leadership's responsibility to accomplish that.

When we interviewed U.S. Army leaders, we wanted to find out how they knew if their knowledge initiatives were working. We asked them what made them think they were having an impact and why they thought they should continue to invest in the Center for Army Lessons Learned. Major Hughes, who works at the center, gave us the best answer. At first he gave us the standard here-is-how-we-measure-it, here-is-how-we-use-it answer. We kept probing and finally, a little frustrated, he said, "You know how I know? I know because Gordon Sullivan, chief of staff of the U.S. Army, uses this stuff. He uses our lessons learned to understand what is happening and to improve his own decision making."

Creating the knowledge engine is too important a task to be left to a technology unit or any other staff unit buried somewhere in the organization or contracted out. The knowledge engine has to be something leaders use to drive their own and their business units' performance. Delegating the responsibility for creating and leveraging knowledge to anyone else will simply not produce the results that you need in today's dynamic economy.

The Role of Leadership

We are definitely facing change, and it is fast, uncharted, and perilous. Yet the role of the leader is much the same as it has always been: to create and capture value. Create value that meets a need, answers a question, and delivers service. Then capture value from what has been created by getting the customer to value it enough to be willing and able to pay for it.

If the basic role of leadership has not changed, what has? Value and competitive advantage are no longer grounded in physical or financial assets. Instead, value comes increasingly from knowledge assets, which have to be created and leveraged. The role of leaders has not changed but the assignments they have to fill their role have. We believe they now have four important assignments.

Assignment 1:
Create a Culture of Observation,
Validation, and Experimentation

Most people are not predisposed to learn and capture knowledge based on their experience. They need a leader to forge the tools and create the techniques, and a culture that will make learning and knowledge capture an expected and natural part of their jobs. They need a culture of observation, validation, and experimentation.

Observation

People need to incorporate reflection into the work process. With the pressure for performance, most of us do not take the time to capture learning. We want to leap back into action. Only if the leader expects us to stop, think, and learn will we learn from our experience. During the U.S. operation in Haiti, each unit commander made sure the unit was doing after action reviews. That is how they started noticing how terrified people were of the military police's big German shepherd dogs. That is what caused them to notice that the local cultural norms excluded women from any type of leadership positions. By turning over command to the women and bringing in the dogs, they very quickly broke the norms and found the guns. At Xerox, everyone is responsible for observing what is happening and capturing lessons learned from their own work and then feeding them into the tips system. In the vast genealogy project, the very process of finding your ancestor adds to the observed knowledge that everyone else on the network can use.

Validation

Does what we see repeat itself? Do other units see the same thing? If so, confidence in our knowledge goes up, and the actions we choose to take are more informed. We reduce the risks and are more aware of the chances we are taking. To validate knowledge, the leader must be both a historian and a scientist. We cannot possibly compare one time period with another unless we have a capture process that gives us comparable information and provides those who work with us access to past documentation.

Everyone has to look for ground truth. But from the leader's vantage point, ground truth varies. For the engineer it may be quite different than for the financial analysts. And so the leader must seek observation and documentation across multiple perspectives. The leader has to be the integrator. Well-designed knowledge banks allow the leader to span the boundaries of multiple units and make validation possible.

In Haiti, for example, the after action reviews, which were done in standard format, were collected and consolidated by observers and sent back to the Center for Army Lessons Learned. The AAR process and CALL's existence now make it possible for leadership at all levels to actively participate in the knowledge creation process.

Experimentation

To determine causality in a world of uncertainty, leaders have to experiment, use their judgment, make choices, and then learn. What happens if we do *A*? Because we do not know, we are best served by getting many different types of experiments going. Each experiment may produce a positive or negative result, but if the learning cycle is fast then the performance can be affected quickly.

People need to feel that they can take risks. But they also need to understand that the risks should pay off in performance and learning. The leader must not only establish the conditions for experimentation but know whether the experiment succeeds or fails. The leader must know what a victory looks like, if what is learned can be used in other places, and when to continue the efforts and transfer what is learned quickly so it can be applied and leveraged in other units. Experimentation produces the knowledge; leverage produces the payoff.

The leader also has another interesting role in experimentation: knowing when and how to kill projects. The test is to move validated knowledge into core knowledge in a world with limited resources. Experiments must increase understanding of what works and why. Poor experiments not only waste time but also create confusion.

Assignment 2:
Get into the Action

Where do you start? The knowledge engine concepts can be applied everywhere in the organization. Each unit has to be aligned with its purpose and be able to learn through experience—that is, have a strategic orientation and a knowledge production capability. The principles are applicable everywhere. You do not have to wait for someone to give you permission or provide resources to begin. You can begin with paper and pencil and a few moments taken to capture the learning. The diagnosis you make will provide you with a sense of where you are weak and where you are strong. It will help you determine the gaps in your knowledge capture and leverage capability. Start where you are weak. Start where you can get payoff. Start where you can leverage. The most important thing, however, is to start. Get into the action today.

Your efforts will most likely go through four phases. Each provides the basis of the next:

⇨ Phase I: Go for quick wins.
⇨ Phase II: Build the knowledge infrastructure.
⇨ Phase III: Leverage knowledge.
⇨ Phase IV: Make creating and leveraging knowledge assets a part of the work process.

Go for Quick Wins

In the first phase, you are trying to identify key business areas where you can produce results with minimal investment and in a short time period. A good test of whether you are focused properly is to look at the people who are supporting your effort. If it is seen as an initiative driven by the business leader you will probably have success. If it is seen as an initiative driven by a staff group, you will have to work harder to gain acceptance.

Often your best hope is to attach an initiative to a project already ongoing in a key business area. That way your effort will automatically be seen as relevant. If you can get the business unit leader excited about the possibilities of helping produce real business results, you are on the right track. You are looking for results in a three-month window. The new economy moves too fast to wait longer.

Build the Knowledge Infrastructure

Once you have results in hand you can start building the infrastructure. You have two main objectives as you begin to build. First, provide a basis to build on what is already known. Each initiative should begin where the previous initiative ended. Each project should be built on the basis of what has already been learned. Second, leverage what you know across the organization. What you learn should have an impact throughout. You can start building an infrastructure that accomplishes both objectives with paper and pencil. Eventually, however, you will want to move to an electronic base to speed up the rate at which knowledge can be captured and shared.

A key issue at this point is scalability. A few isolated groups effectively sharing knowledge are not likely to make an impact on a large organization. When something that works is discovered, the infrastructure must allow it to be driven quickly through the other units.

Leverage Knowledge

With the infrastructure in place and early successes known, the key leadership challenge is to leverage the knowledge. Enroll a broader coalition of leaders who are willing to use it. In turn, they have to encourage local experimentation, bring people and units together to discuss success and failures, and create an incubator to share technology and reuse processes, tools, and methods. Most of all, they have to recognize and reward success.

The first questions to ask should focus on building on past knowledge. For example, "How does this build on what others have done?" or "Are we sure we have not already done something in this area that we should be building on?" In reality it does little good for one unit to learn something; the power is gained as knowledge is leveraged across multiple units. The second questions deal with leverage after the project. "Who else needs to know what you have learned?" and "How are you going to get what they need to them?"

This is also the phase at which you can begin increasing your investment in technology—now you know where the payoff is likely to be. It is a good idea to wait until this third phase to do so, because of the potential of wasting large sums of money in areas where knowledge has no impact. All you have to do is look around your own organization at the junkyard of technology to find technology investments that have not lived up to their promises. In fact, a good objective is to make sure that expenditures are so integrated into the ongoing operations of the firm that they are not considered separately.

Make Creating and Leveraging
Knowledge Assets a Part of the Work Process

Capturing and leveraging knowledge should be made into an ongoing part of the work process. It simply must become a way of life. Every assignment becomes not only an opportunity to perform but also an opportunity to learn. Every project is a test to see how it can be done better. Every customer transaction becomes a source of new knowledge. You can test whether this is the case by assessing your current work structures. To what extent do they leverage actual, real-time lessons learned from one unit back into other units? How well do communities work together to focus and drive knowledge-sharing activities? How well does the firm use peers and experts to review plans and help capture learning? Is top management engaged and do they really use the knowledge created? Asking these types of questions will go a long way in determining if knowledge sharing is part of your culture.

Leaders can also affect what people do with the reward structure. People do what they are rewarded to do. They focus on what is measured and what the top of the organization values. Performance management systems have to value and reward knowledge management. Those who get ahead should be seen as those who affect performance beyond their own unit. Promotions should go to those who not only can learn quickly but also can help others learn quickly. Incentives must be based on accomplishing business objectives and leveraging knowledge.

Assignment 3:
Move from Managing the Plan
to Managing the Net

In the hierarchical world of the industrial past, planning, implementation, and thinking occurred in a linear sequence. Management by Objectives was born in the 1960s and lives on. Set the goal, determine the action plan, define the metrics, and then work toward your goal. It worked well in a world where change was slow and linear. However, we live in a world that is fast and *hyperlinked*. The best way to understand a hyperlinked world is to watch a group of kids today do a research report. When most of us were growing up that meant going to the library and spending hours searching through catalogues to find the information we needed. We sifted and sorted and finally compiled the information into a report with background, thesis, data, conclusion, and recommendations. Today, kids sit at a computer to search. As they read about one topic, key words, phrases, and concepts automatically link them to other topics. They find an important issue, click on it, and are off into another report. In that report they will hit other concepts linked to even more sites and concepts. Because of the speed and flexibility with which they can move, they can search many related topics. Imagine what these kids are going to do in organizations when they go to work. Imagine the type of leadership they will demand. They will not want planners and controllers. They will want teachers, experimenters, and relationship builders.

The hyperlinked world is already beginning to affect the products and services that organizations provide and how they operate. For example, log onto **Edmunds.com** and look at the extensive car-buying services. This massive set of data is available not only to consumers with Web sites linked together but also to dealers, so they can track what customers are asking for and what they are buying. The consumers control the nature of the search process and can quickly find what they want. The producers not only fill customer needs more quickly but also track how customers are searching and what questions they are asking. At Fidelity, when customers have a question about their retirement policies, they can quickly search through all of Fidelity's extensive information and information from many other sources, which is linked to Fidelity's information. Slowly but surely the customers are even beginning to link with each other and becoming a customer community that will drive what Fidelity does and how it does it. Hierarchical ways of thinking, acting, and leading will not work in the nonlinear, hyperlinked world. You not only have to maintain the complex web of relationships that allows you to meet the customer's needs but also have to be able to reconfigure the web as situations change.

As we form partnerships, alliances, and linkages we become more dependent on each other. Vertical integration was the watch cry of the industrial economy. Control as much of the basics of production as you possibly can. Be independent of all. If you must rely on suppliers, make sure you have solid contracts and can control them as much as possible. In the new economy the leadership challenge is to focus on relationships. What do you do well and how can you leverage that? How can you form good working relationships with others? Success in the new economy will be determined by how well you maintain your relationships. How will you build a port-folio of capabilities through the relationships you maintain? There is a clear movement away from vertical integration toward greater reliance on components produced by others. And yet each firm and individual must sustain their cores. Leadership must focus on identifying and building that core and putting in place the learning process that will sustain it.

Assignment 4:
Integrate Knowledge and Development

Knowledge initiatives and personal development are often seen as two separate things. The first is run by the information technology department and the second by human resources. Some organizations are trying to bring them together but are only partially succeeding. They spend their time trying to bring the knowledge into the learning process. They bring organization problems into the classroom. They adopt action learning programs, and convene groups to help them get up to speed on their skills, and give them work-related assignments. Most recently, they go to online learning. They provide learning on demand, so people can ask for help and get it when and where they need it. With all of these efforts, they are trying to get more performance into the learning process. They identify the skills needed to perform, identify the learning agenda, structure the development experience, and help develop the skills. All of this helps, but often it does not happen fast enough or is not grounded enough in performance to keep up with the pace of change.

Technology allows new and exciting ways of getting more performance into the learning process. Consider, for example, students in a classroom discussing a case that involves product introduction and marketing who are linked to real time data, actions, and knowledge. They have the opportunity not only to see and use real time data from after action reviews, project evaluations, and current strategic planning to develop their own decisions but also to comment and give input. The "ah-ha's" made during the discussions in the learning environment can be fed right back into the performance process for those who are performing to consider. Their new perspective often adds tremendous insight to problems that those directly involved in the situation cannot resolve.

If we shift our perspective from getting more performance into the learning process to getting more learning into the performance process, a whole new set of development approaches can be added. Performing and learning are not sequential but simultaneous. Learning is a by-product of performance. The most common methods we have found to get more learning into the performance process are after action reviews, learning observers, and reflection.

You can also run experiments to see what happens. For example, your total marketing plan may be based on a product development and introduction cycle that assumes three years from inception to introduction. What would happen if that were cut in half? How would that change affect the supply chain, the recruiting process, the financials, and so on? You can introduce that change into a simulation and see what happens to the production cycles, the financial systems, the personnel network; you can watch in a compressed time what executives and managers actually do if you change some critical parameters of the organizations—all in an effort to better integrate development and knowledge.

It Starts and Ends with the Leader

Because this point is so important, it needs to be highlighted again: *It all starts and ends with the leader.* Knowledge assets begin with the leader who focuses efforts on business purposes. The leader has to define the focus of any knowledge initiative. What is the payoff? A little money spent in the right area has a far greater impact than large amounts scattered throughout the corporation. The process ends with the leader who consolidates, validates, and integrates. The leader has to combine perspectives from multiple sources to gain an overall view. Focusing and reflecting are the beginning and the ending of the process, where leaders establish and maintain the strategic orientation and produce business results.

Those leaders who learn how to create and leverage knowledge assets will give their organizations a definite competitive advantage. But shifting one's mindset is a hard thing to do. We grew up in a world where our models of business and leadership were based on physical and financial assets. Although still very important, as the world continues to change these assets will simply bring parity with others. Real value will be created and captured by those who understand how to lead from a base of knowledge.

As we said back in Chapter 1, we chose to use the word *leader* in this book rather than *top executive* because not only those at the top of the organization have the responsibility or the opportunity to make an impact. The responsibility lies with every type of leader throughout the organization, from the unit head to the leader of the accounting team to the project coordinator. Eventually every individual becomes a leader, because everyone has leadership responsibilities.

In the future, leadership will continue to be about vision, integration, and implementation. But more and more it will also be about knowledge. Can you create and leverage knowledge assets? Can you learn from your own experiences? Can you structure what you know so others have easy access and want to take what you have learned into their situation? Can you deliver the right knowledge to the right person in the right format at the right time? Can you step back, take a higher-level view, and consolidate learning to drive strategic change? Focus, acquire, structure, target, and reflect.

And then do it all over again.

References

Abraham, H. (2000, Oct. 4). *Presentation to the Leadership Institute*. Boston University, Boston.

Argyris, C. (1977, Sept.-Oct.). "Double-Loop Learning in Organizations." *Harvard Business Review*, pp. 115–124.

Baird, L., and Henderson, J. (1997, Winter). "Learning from Action: An Analysis of the Center for Army Lessons Learned (CALL)." *Human Resource Management, 36*(4), 385–395.

Baird, L., Holland, P., and Deacon, S. (1999, Spring). "Learning from Action: Embedding More Learning into the Performance Fast Enough to Make a Difference." *Organizational Dynamics*, pp. 19–32.

Baldwin, C., and Clark, K. (1997, Sept.-Oct.)."Managing in an Age of Modularity." *Harvard Business Review*, pp. 84–93.

Boulding, K. E. (1953). *The Organizational Revolution: A Study in the Ethics of Economic Organization*. New York: Harper & Row.

Bradley, S., and Nolan, R. (1998). *Sense and Respond: Capturing Value in the Network Era*. Boston: Harvard Business School Press.

Broadbent, M., and Weill, P. (1997, Spring). "Management by Maxim: How Business and IT Managers Can Create IT Infrastructures." *Sloan Management Review, 38*(3).

Christensen, C. (1997). *The Innovator's Dilemma: Where New Technologies Cause Great Firms to Fail*. Boston: Harvard Business School Press.

Churchman, C. (1983). *The Systems Approach*. New York: Dell.

Covey, S. (1990). *The Seven Habits of Highly Effective People*. New York: Simon & Schuster.

Daudelin, M. (1996, Winter). "Learning from Experience Through Reflection." *Organizational Dynamics*, pp. 36–48.

Davenport, T., and Prusak, L. (1998). *Working Knowledge*. Boston: Harvard Business School Press.

Deacon, S. (1998, May). *Field Notes from Phillips Petroleum*.

Evans, P., and Wurster, T. (2000). *Blown to Bits: How the New Economics of Information Transforms Strategy*. Boston: Harvard Business School Press.

Fine, C. *Clockspeed*. (1998). Boston: Perseus Books.

Goldberg, D., Nichols, B., Oki, B. M., and Terry, D. (1992). "Using Collaborative Filtering to Weave an Information Tapestry." *Communications of the ACM, 35*, 61–70 .

Greiner, L. (1998, May-June). "Evolution and Revolution as Organizations Grow." *Harvard Business Review*, p. 64.

Griffin, D. (1999, May 25). *Presentation to the Executive Development Roundtable*. Boston University, Boston.

Haeckel, S. (1999). *Adaptive Enterprise: Creating and Leading Sense and Respond Organization*. Boston: Harvard Business School Press.

Hartman, A., Sifonis, J. and Kafdor, J. (2000). *Net Ready*. New York: McGraw-Hill.

Hayes, R., Wheelwright, S., and Clark, K. (1988). "Laying the Foundation for Product and Process Development." In Hayes, Wheelwright, and Clark, *Dynamic Manufacturing* (pp. 273–303). New York: Free Press.

Heifetz, R. A. (1994). *Leadership Without Easy Answers*. Boston: Belknap Press.

Kuhn, T. S. (1976). *The Structure of Scientific Revolutions*, 2nd ed., enlarged. Chicago: University of Chicago Press.

Lancet (1994). Randomised trial of cholesterol lowering in 4444 patients with coronary heart disease: the Scandinavian Simvastatin Survival Study (4S), November 19, pp. 1383–1389.

Maes, P., Guttman, R. H., and Moukas, A. G. (1999). "Agents That Buy and Sell." *Communications of the ACM, 42*(3), 81.

Mason, R., and Mitroff, I. (1981). *Challenging Strategic Planning Assumptions: Theory, Cases, and Techniques.* New York: Wiley.

Nonaka, L., and Takeuchi, H. (1995). *The Knowledge-Creating Company.* New York: Oxford University Press.

Parcell, G., and Milton, N. (n.d.). *Peer Assists: Learning Before, During, and After: Knowledge Management Tools for BP* (brochure).

Pearse, K., and Parcell, G. (1998). *After Action Reviews: Knowledge Management Tools for BP* (brochure).

Peppers, D., and Rogers, M. (1999). *Enterprise One to One: Tools for Competing in the Interactive Age.* New York: Doubleday.

Pine, B. (1999). *Mass Customization: The New Frontier in Business Competition.* Boston: Harvard Business School Press.

Prokesch, S. (1997). "Unleashing the Power of Learning: An Interview with British Petroleum's John Browne." *Harvard Business Review, 75*(5), 4–19.

Quinn, J. B. (1992). *Intelligent Enterprise.* New York: Free Press.

Rockart, J. (1979, Mar.-Apr.). "Chief Executives Define Their Own Data Needs." *Harvard Business Review,* pp. 81–93.

Schon, D. (1984). *The Reflective Practitioner.* Chicago: University of Chicago Press.

Slocum, J. W. Jr., McGill, M., and Lei, D. T. (1994, Autumn). "The New Learning Strategy: Anytime, Anything, Anywhere." *Organizational Dynamics, 23*(2), 33–47.

Spear, S., and Bowen, H. K. (1999, Sept.-Oct.) "Deciding the DNA of the Toyota Production System." *Harvard Business Review,* pp. 97–106.

Storck, J., and Hill, P. (2000, Winter). "Knowledge Diffusion Through

Strategic Communities." *Sloan Management Review, 41*(2), 63.

Sullivan, G. (1998, May 21). *Presentation to the Executive Development Roundtable.* Boston University, Boston.

Sullivan, G., and Harper, M. (1997). *Hope Is Not a Method.* New York: Broadway Books.

U.S. Army. (1993). *A Leader's Guide to After Action Reviews.* Washington, D.C.: U.S. Army.

Venables, M. (1999, May 25). *Presentation to the Executive Development Roundtable.* Boston University, Boston.

Venkatraman, N. (1999, May 12). *Presentation to the Systems Research Center.* Boston University, Boston.

Venkatraman, N., and Henderson, J. (1998, Fall). "Real Strategies for Virtual Organizing." *Sloan Management Review, 40*(1), 49.

Weick, K. E. (1995). *Sensemaking in Organizations.* Thousand Oaks, CA: Sage.

PERFORMANCE

Index

KNOWLEDGE

About the Authors

LLOYD BAIRD is professor of management at Boston University and executive director of the Leadership Institute, which he helped found. He is currently a principal at the Systems Research Center and research director of the Executive Development Roundtable, where he focuses on the role of top executives and executive development. Each of these groups brings together leading organizations to work on common issues and problems. Together they include over one hundred corporations that are devoted to remaining on the cutting edge of practice.

In working with many corporations, Baird has been able to do a full analysis of the corporation and help them understand the risks and the potential of corporatewide learning, knowledge, and technology initiatives that are designed to drive performance and bring the culture into alignment with the strategy. He also works with executives to help them lead both personal and organization transformation. He is currently helping firms leverage their executive development activities.

In addition to his work with firms, Baird is actively participating in, directing, and managing several other consortia of corporations. He is a principal at the Center for Enterprise Leadership, a collection of twenty-five corporations that jointly sponsor consulting and research in operations, and he is involved in the Human Resources Policy Institute. He is the author of numerous books and articles on the topics of human resource management and executive development.

Baird received his B.S. degree from Utah State University and his M.B.A. and Ph.D. from Michigan State University.

JOHN C. HENDERSON is chair of the Management Information Systems Department at Boston University's School of Management and is also the director of the Systems Research Center and the Richard G. Shipley Endowed Chair. At the Systems Research Center he is involved with top corporations globally, developing and implementing corporate information technology strategy and most recently developing strategies and applications that fit a faster moving, dynamic economy. He is a noted researcher, consultant, and executive educator with published papers appearing in journals such as *Management Science, Sloan Management Review, MIS Quarterly, IBM Systems Journal, European Management Journal,* and many others. He is often sought out for editorial comment in academic and applied journals and is popular with journalists as one who understands both the worlds of theory and application.

Working with colleagues from multiple disciplines he currently serves as director of the Institute for Leading in a Dynamic Economy.

Presently Henderson's research focuses on three main areas: managing strategic partnerships, aligning business and information technology strategies, and strategy formulation. He has served on the editorial boards of the *Journal of Management Information Systems, Decision Sciences,* and *Management Science,* where he was the departmental editor. Prior to joining Boston University, he served on the faculty at the MIT Sloan School of Management. He received his Ph.D. from the University of Texas at Austin.

Berrett-Koehler Publishers

BERRETT-KOEHLER is an independent publisher of books, periodicals, and other publications at the leading edge of new thinking and innovative practice on work, business, management, leadership, stewardship, career development, human resources, entrepreneurship, and global sustainability.

Since the company's founding in 1992, we have been committed to supporting the movement toward a more enlightened world of work by publishing books, periodicals, and other publications that help us to integrate our values with our work and work lives, and to create more humane and effective organizations.

We have chosen to focus on the areas of work, business, and organizations, because these are central elements in many people's lives today. Furthermore, the work world is going through tumultuous changes, from the decline of job security to the rise of new structures for organizing people and work. We believe that change is needed at all levels— individual, organizational, community, and global—and our publications address each of these levels.

We seek to create new lenses for understanding organizations, to legitimize topics that people care deeply about but that current business orthodoxy censors or considers secondary to bottom-line concerns, and to uncover new meaning, means, and ends for our work and work lives.

See next pages for other books from Berrett-Koehler Publishers

More books from Berrett-Koehler

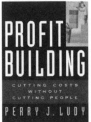

Profit Building
Cutting Costs Without Cutting People

Perry Ludy

In *Profit Building,* Perry Ludy—who has worked for top companies in every major field from manufacturing to retail—introduces a five-step process called the PBP (Profit Building Process), which offers specific techniques for improving profitability by stimulating creative thinking and motivating teams to work together more effectively.

Hardcover, 200 pages • ISBN 1-57675-108-2 CIP
Item #51082-363 $27.95

Corporate Creativity
How Innovation and Improvement Actually Happen

Alan G. Robinson and Sam Stern

Alan Robinson and Sam Stern have investigated hundreds of creative acts that have occurred in organizations around the world to find the truth about how innovation and improvement really happen. Rich with detailed examples, *Corporate Creativity* identifies six essential elements that companies can use to turn their creativity from a hit-or-miss proposition into something consistent that they can count on.

Paperback, 300 pages • ISBN 1-57675-049-3 CIP
Item #50493-363 $17.95

Hardcover • ISBN 1-57675-009-4 CIP • Item #50094-363 $29.95

Audiotape, 2 cassettes/3 hrs. • ISBN 1-56511-264-4
Item #12644-363 $16.95

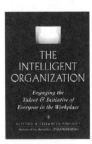

The Intelligent Organization
Engaging the Talent and Initiative of Everyone in the Workplace

Gifford and Elizabeth Pinchot

The Pinchots show how, by developing and engaging the intelligence, business judgment, and wide-system responsibility of all its members, an organization can respond more effectively to customers, partners, and competitors.

Paperback, 420 pages • ISBN 1-881052-98-2 CIP
Item #52982-363 $19.95

Hardcover • ISBN 1-881052-34-6 CIP • Item #52346-363 $24.95

Berrett-Koehler Publishers PO Box 565, Williston, VT 05495-9900
Call toll-free! **800-929-2929** 7 am-12 midnight

BK Or fax your order to 802-864-7627
For fastest service order online: **www.bkconnection.com**

Smart Thinking for Crazy Times
The Art of Solving the Right Problems

Ian Mitroff

The ability to spot the right problems, frame them correctly, and implement appropriate solutions is the true competitive edge that will separate the successful individuals and organizations from the also-rans. Here, Ian Mitroff shows how to cut through complex issues, ask the right questions, and solve the right problems.

Hardcover, 200 pages • ISBN 1-57675-020-5 CIP
Item #50205-363 $24.95

Audiotape, 1 cassette/90 mins. • ISBN 0-78711-727-7
Item #17277-363 $13.00

Images of Organization
—The Executive Edition

Gareth Morgan

Recognized as one of the most influential management texts of the last decade, *Images of Organization* revolutionized the way we look at organizations. Now this classic book has been revised, updated, and abridged to meet the needs of today's managers.

Hardcover, 400 pages • ISBN 1-57675-038-8 CIP
Item #50388-363 $35.00

Imaginization
New Mindsets for Seeing, Organizing, and Managing

Gareth Morgan

"Imaginization" is a way of thinking and organizing. It is a key managerial skill that will help you develop your creative potential, and find innovative solutions to difficult problems. It answers the call for more creative forms of organization and management. Imaginization shows how to put this approach into practice.

Paperback, 350 pages • ISBN 1-57675-026-4 CIP
Item #50264-363 $19.95

Berrett-Koehler Publishers PO Box 565, Williston, VT 05495-9900
Call toll-free! **800-929-2929** 7 am-12 midnight

BK Or fax your order to 802-864-7627
For fastest service order online: **www.bkconnection.com**

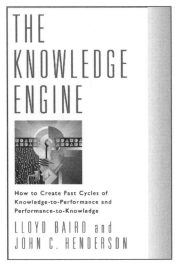